THE AUSTRALIAN **Women's Weekly**

ONE POT

THE AUSTRALIAN **Women's Weekly**

ONE POT

WHOLESOME, TIME-SAVING
EVERYDAY RECIPES

Project Editor Emma Hill
Project Designer Alison Shackleton
Editorial Assistant Kiron Gill
Jacket Designer Alison Donovan
Jackets Coordinator Lucy Philpott
Production Editor Heather Blagden
Senior Producer Luca Bazzoli
Creative Technical Support Sonia Charbonnier
Managing Editor Dawn Henderson
Managing Art Editor Alison Donovan
Art Director Maxine Pedliham
Publishing Director Katie Cowan

First published in Great Britain in 2021
by Dorling Kindersley Limited
DK, One Embassy Gardens, 8 Viaduct Gardens, London, SW11 7BW

The authorised representative in the EEA is Dorling Kindersley
Verlag GmbH. Arnulfstr. 124, 80636 Munich, Germany

A CIP catalogue record for this book is available from the British Library.
ISBN: 978-0-2415-1017-9

Printed and bound in China

For the curious
www.dk.com

MIX
Paper from
responsible sources
FSC™ C018179

This book was made with Forest Stewardship Council ™ certified paper –
one small step in DK's commitment to a sustainable future.
For more information go to **www.dk.com/our-green-pledge**

Contents

One-pot cooking

You only need one piece of equipment to whip up these brilliant one-pot dishes, guaranteed to satisfy the entire family. So break out your saucepan, frying pan, wok, or baking dish.

Saucepans

The ideal saucepan has sturdy sides as well as a heavy, thick base and a tight-fitting lid. Good saucepans are heavy because they have thick bases to hold the heat and spread it evenly. A top-quality saucepan can cook evenly over a low heat, without the food scorching or sticking, for a long period. Judge a saucepan by its weight and the material it is made of. A good saucepan must respond quickly when heat is increased or decreased, and this depends on whether it is made of material that is a good conductor or a poor one. Different metals, or combinations of metals, of which saucepans are made, have a great effect on how they perform. So too does the size.

Saucepans are designed to hold a much deeper mass of food than frying pans, and cook the food by surrounding it with even, moist heat. Tall saucepans conserve moisture, so they are well-suited to long, slow cooking. Wide saucepans, especially those with slightly outward-sloping sides, are easy to see into and their bases are wide enough to brown food properly. Wide saucepans, rather than tall ones are also better suited for reducing or simmering a sauce, as the large surface of the base helps evaporation.

Frying pans

The first thing to look for in a frying pan is not how it looks, but how it feels in your hand. A medium-sized frying pan (20–22cm across the base) is the most useful. If you need greater capacity, a second medium pan provides more versatility and easier handling than having just one very large pan. Check the base is cast (shaped in a mould in one piece) and ground flat so that it never warps. It must be thick so that it will take up and hold the heat.

In order to perform well, a pan must be made of material that is a good conductor – that transmits heat evenly to the whole cooking surface, and responds quickly when the heat is turned up or down. The handle should feel comfortable to your hand and well-balanced with the weight of the frying pan. Riveted or welded-on handles are better. A handle that can go into the oven makes a frying pan more useful. A lid is also useful because browning is often only the first step in a recipe, to be followed by covered cooking. Both the handle and lid knob should stay cool enough to pick up without a pot-holder during stovetop cooking (though remember that they will get too hot to handle in the oven without the protection of a cloth).

Many frying pans are available with non-stick coatings, but these reduce conductivity and so the pan's ability to brown well. These finishes don't usually last well; they get worn and scratched during the speedy action that frying calls for, and suffer from exposure to high heat. While some manufacturer's recommend using moderate temperatures only, high heat is needed to sear meats and vegetables to a delicious brown crustiness on the outside without overcooking the interior.

Woks

The wok evolved over the centuries as the most efficient design for cooking over flames. Stir-frying, the technique used most often in wok-cooking, remains the perfect way to cook over a very high heat in a very short time. Stir-frying works better on gas burners than on electric ones, because gas flames surround the wok with the intense heat needed for short cooking times. Some woks have flat bottoms, which make the wok stand straight on an electric or ceramic burner without support, but this defeats the purpose of the classic design, which is to concentrate intense heat at the centre. Some have non-stick linings, which are not suitable for cooking on high heat, and electric woks don't get hot enough. Choose a wok made from carbon steel rather than stainless steel or aluminium. Cooks often prefer a cast-iron wok for stir-frying on an electric stove because it holds the heat better than carbon-steel.

Baking dishes

There are many ovenproof baking dishes in various shapes and sizes, from soufflé dishes and pie dishes to casseroles and gratin dishes. Here, we are talking about the shallow oven dishes you reach for when you want to make lasagne, moussaka, bread and butter pudding, or to bake stuffed apples, tomatoes, or capsicums (peppers).

Good baking dishes are deep enough to accommodate the layers of a lasagne, while their large surface areas encourage evaporation, so the finished dish will be moist but not wet, and delicately golden on top. Consider the quantities you will be cooking when choosing an ovenproof baking dish. A good baking dish should feel heavy for its size because it is made from metal thick enough to resist warping and hot spots. Plain aluminium, or, even better, because it is stronger, an aluminium alloy, are the choices of many chefs. These pans are heavy enough, but not too heavy, and perform better on top of the stove than stainless-steel pans, which look smarter but can't match aluminium's superb conductivity. Ceramic ovenproof dishes work equally well, especially when roasting tomato-based dishes. Baking dishes are also available in enamelled cast iron, which has the advantage over the other materials for being dishwasher safe. These dishes are also suitable for serving food such as a lasagne at the table. A baking dish that can also be used on a stove is especially helpful.

SAUCEPAN

You can create a wonderful array of dishes using just one pot, from warming curries and stews to noodle soups, tagines, and elegant seafood bowls.

Creamy potato and leek soup

PREP + COOK TIME **30 MINUTES** | SERVES **2**

This soup is brimming with flavour and makes a perfect warming starter or lunch on a chilly day. Cheese and prosciutto toasts served alongside take this soup course to another level. Comfort food at its finest.

1 tsp extra virgin olive oil

1 garlic clove, coarsely chopped

1 small leek (200g), white part only, coarsely chopped

1 trimmed celery stalk (100g), coarsely chopped

2 medium potatoes (400g), diced into 1cm pieces

1 tbsp fresh lemon thyme leaves

3 cups (750ml) chicken or vegetable stock

1/3 cup (80ml) pouring (single) cream

salt and freshly ground black pepper

lemon thyme leaves, extra to serve

cheese and prosciutto toasts (optional)

1 tsp extra virgin olive oil

2 slices prosciutto (30g)

4 slices sourdough bread (200g)

1/2 cup (60g) grated vintage cheddar

1 Heat the olive oil in a medium saucepan over a medium heat. Add the garlic, leek, celery, potato, and thyme; cook, stirring, for 2 minutes or until the leek softens.

2 Add the stock and cream to the pan, bring to the boil, reduce the heat; simmer, covered, for 15 minutes or until the vegetables are softened. Season with salt and pepper to taste. Stand for 10 minutes.

3 Make the cheese and prosciutto toasts. Place the prosciutto and bread on an oven tray lined with baking paper; top the bread with the cheddar. Cook in the oven at 200°C (180°C fan/400°F/Gas 6) for 8 minutes or until the cheddar has melted and the prosciutto is crisp. Top the cheese toast with the crumbled prosciutto.

4 Blend or process the soup until smooth. Season with freshly ground black pepper. Serve the soup sprinkled with lemon thyme leaves and the cheese toasts on the side, if you like.

TIP

This soup can be made a day ahead; reheat just before serving, while cooking the prosciutto and cheddar toasts.

Chicken, bacon, and mushroom stew

PREP + COOK TIME **2 HOURS 15 MINUTES** | SERVES **6**

Letting this traditional French stew bubble away on a low heat intensifies the flavours of the full-bodied sauce beautifully. Serve for a warming and hearty supper with mashed potatoes and green vegetables, if you like.

1 tbsp olive oil

350g streaky bacon slices, cut widthways into thin strips

12 chicken legs (1.5kg)

2 medium leeks (700g), white part only, thinly sliced

400g button mushrooms, trimmed

3 garlic cloves, crushed

2 tbsp plain flour

1/2 cup (125ml) dry white wine

2 cups (500ml) chicken stock

2 tbsp wholegrain mustard

2 tbsp fresh thyme leaves, plus extra to serve

salt and freshly ground black pepper

sour cream, to serve (optional)

1 Heat the olive oil in a 5-litre (20-cup) flameproof casserole dish or stew pan (see tips) over a medium-high heat. Cook the bacon, stirring, for 5 minutes or until golden and crisp. Transfer to a large plate.

2 Cook the chicken in the casserole dish, in batches, turning, for 10 minutes or until browned all over; transfer each batch to the plate with the bacon.

3 Add the leek and mushrooms to the casserole dish; cook, stirring, for 5 minutes or until softened. Add the garlic and flour; cook, stirring, for 30 seconds or until the mixture looks dry. Gradually stir in the wine, stock, mustard, and thyme. Return the chicken and bacon to the dish; bring to the boil. Reduce the heat to low; cook, covered, for 1 1/2 hours or until the chicken is very tender. Season with salt and pepper to taste.

4 Serve half the chicken stew topped with the extra thyme and sour cream, if using. Transfer the remaining chicken stew to an airtight container; cool, then store in the refrigerator (see tips).

TIPS

- We used a 26cm round cast iron casserole dish.
- You can refrigerate the chicken stew in an airtight container for up to 2 days.
- The stew can be frozen for up to 3 months; thaw in the fridge, then reheat in a microwave.

Green curry and makrut lime prawn soup

PREP + COOK TIME **45 MINUTES** | SERVES **4**

This fresh and spicy Thai noodle soup not only looks stunning, but is bursting with brilliantly zingy flavours. Light, refreshing, and perfectly balanced, creamy coconut milk and green curry paste form the base for the classic Thai flavour triptych of sweet, spicy, and sour.

1kg uncooked medium prawns

1 tbsp peanut oil

1/4 cup (75g) green curry paste

1 litre (4 cups) chicken stock

2 x 400ml can coconut milk

1 fresh long green chilli, finely chopped

8 fresh makrut lime leaves

125g rice vermicelli

125g sugar snap peas, trimmed, halved lengthways

2 tbsp grated palm sugar

2 tbsp lime juice

2 tbsp fish sauce

salt and freshly ground black pepper

1 cup (80g) bean sprouts

1/2 cup (4g) loosely packed Vietnamese mint leaves (see tip)

1 fresh long green chilli, extra, thinly sliced

2 limes, cut into thin wedges

1 Shell and devein the prawns, leaving the tails intact. Heat the peanut oil in a large saucepan over a medium heat; cook the prawns, in batches, for 2 minutes or until lightly browned. Remove from the pan.

2 Add the curry paste to the same pan; cook, stirring, for about 2 minutes or until fragrant. Add the stock, coconut milk, chopped chilli, and 4 crushed lime leaves; bring to the boil. Reduce the heat; simmer, uncovered, for 20 minutes. Return the prawns to the pan with the vermicelli and peas; cook, uncovered, until the vermicelli is just tender. Stir in the sugar, lime juice, and fish sauce. Season with salt and pepper to taste.

3 Finely shred the remaining lime leaves. Serve the soup sprinkled with the shredded lime leaves, bean sprouts, mint leaves, and sliced chilli. Serve with lime wedges.

TIP

Vietnamese mint is not a mint, but a narrow-leafed, pungent herb, also known as laksa leaf.

Vegetable minestrone

VEGETARIAN | PREP + COOK TIME **50 MINUTES** | SERVES **6**

This is a speedier vegetarian version of the Italian classic, which usually uses dried beans and ham hocks and requires long cooking times. You could use a can of red kidney beans if you can't find canned borlotti beans. Serve with crusty bread.

1 tbsp olive oil

1 medium onion (150g), coarsely chopped

1 garlic clove, crushed

$1/4$ cup (70g) tomato paste

1.5 litres (6 cups) water

2 cups (500ml) vegetable stock

$2^2/_3$ cups (700g) bottled tomato passata

1 celery stalk (150g), trimmed, finely chopped

1 medium carrot (120g), finely chopped

1 medium courgette (120g), finely chopped

80g green beans, trimmed, sliced diagonally

400g can borlotti beans, drained, rinsed

$3/4$ cup (135g) macaroni

salt and freshly ground black pepper

$1/3$ cup coarsely chopped fresh basil leaves

1 Heat the olive oil in a large saucepan; cook the onion and garlic, stirring, for 5 minutes or until the onion softens. Add the tomato paste; cook, stirring, for 2 minutes. Add the water, stock, and passata; bring to the boil.

2 Add the celery to the pan; simmer for 10 minutes. Add the carrot, courgette, and green beans; simmer for 20 minutes or until the carrot is tender. Add the borlotti beans and macaroni; simmer for 10 minutes or until the pasta is tender. Season with salt and pepper to taste.

3 Serve the soup topped with basil and shaved parmesan, if you like.

TIP

For an even quicker version, use 2 cups (250g) frozen mixed diced vegetables instead of the fresh vegetables added in step 2.

Lemongrass prawn and pea curry

PREP + COOK TIME **45 MINUTES** | SERVES **4**

Making your own curry paste from scratch is simpler than you may think and will bring vibrancy and freshness to this fragrant Thai curry. This stunning dish is sure to enliven the tastebuds and impress your guests. Serve with steamed jasmine rice.

1 tbsp vegetable oil

2 cups (500ml) chicken stock

1 cup (250ml) coconut milk

1 tbsp fish sauce

2 tbsp brown sugar

2 tbsp lime juice

800g uncooked medium tiger prawns

1 cup (120g) frozen peas

salt and freshly ground black pepper

1 lime, cut into wedges

lemongrass curry paste

10cm stick fresh lemongrass (20g)

6cm piece fresh ginger (30g)

1 bunch fresh coriander (100g), with roots attached

1 fresh small Thai green chilli, coarsely chopped

2 shallots (50g), coarsely chopped

2 garlic cloves, coarsely chopped

2 tbsp water

1 Make the lemongrass curry paste. Trim the lemongrass; chop coarsely. Peel the ginger; slice thickly. Wash the coriander roots and stems; chop coarsely (you need 2 tablespoons). Pick $1/4$ cup (4g) of coriander leaves; reserve remaining leaves for serving. Blend or process the lemongrass, ginger, coriander root and stem mixture, coriander leaves, chilli, shallot, garlic, and water until smooth, or pound all these ingredients to a paste in a mortar and pestle.

2 Heat the oil in a large saucepan; cook the curry paste, stirring, until fragrant. Add the stock, coconut milk, fish sauce, sugar, and lime juice; simmer for 5 minutes.

3 Meanwhile, shell and devein the prawns leaving the tails intact. Add the prawns and peas to the pan; simmer for 3 minutes or until the prawns change colour. Season with salt and pepper to taste.

4 Sprinkle the curry with the reserved coriander leaves; serve with lime wedges.

Chicken and seafood tomato rice

PREP + COOK TIME **1 HOUR** | SERVES **6**

The combination of chicken and seafood in this recipe makes it reminiscent of the eternally popular Spanish one-pot classic, paella. This recipe is slightly simpler but just as delicious. Serve with a leafy green salad, if you like.

500g uncooked medium king prawns

2 tbsp olive oil

600g chicken thigh fillets, coarsely chopped

1 medium onion (150g), finely chopped

3 garlic cloves, thinly sliced

$1/2$ tsp dried chilli flakes

1 tsp smoked paprika

$1^1/2$ cups (300g) white medium-grain rice

2 x 400g can chopped tomatoes

$2^1/2$ cups (625ml) chicken stock

500g baby clams

salt and freshly ground black pepper

$1/4$ cup coarsely chopped fresh flat-leaf parsley

1 medium lemon (140g), cut into wedges

1   Shell and devein the prawns, leaving the tails intact. Heat the olive oil in a large saucepan; cook the chicken then the prawns, in batches, until almost cooked through. Remove from the pan.

2   Add the onion to the same pan; cook, stirring, for 5 minutes or until softened.

3   Add the garlic to the pan with the chilli flakes and paprika. Cook, stirring, until fragrant. Add the rice, tomatoes, and stock; bring to the boil. Reduce the heat; simmer, covered, for 25 minutes.

4   Return the chicken and prawns to the pan with the clams; simmer, covered, for 10 minutes or until the rice is tender and the clams open. Season with salt and pepper to taste.

5   Sprinkle the rice with parsley; serve with lemon wedges.

TIP

Some clams might not open after cooking. These may need prompting with a knife or might not have cooked as quickly as the others – you do not have to discard these, just open with a knife and cook a little more if you wish.

Meatball tagine with baked eggs

PREP + COOK TIME **1 HOUR** | SERVES **4**

Baked eggs are a delicious breakfast food, and here we adapt them to be a filling protein-rich
dinner with the inclusion of the spiced meatballs. Serve this tagine with Greek-style yogurt
and grilled pitta bread to soak up the sauce.

500g minced beef

1 garlic clove, crushed

1/4 cup (12g) finely chopped fresh mint

2 tbsp finely chopped fresh coriander

1 tsp ground cinnamon

1 tsp ground coriander

2 tsp ground cumin

1/2 tsp chilli powder

salt and freshly ground black pepper

1 tbsp olive oil

1 medium onion (150g), finely chopped

4 large tomatoes (880g), coarsely chopped

pinch saffron threads

4 eggs

1/2 cup (8g) fresh coriander leaves

1 Combine the beef, garlic, mint, chopped coriander, cinnamon, ground
coriander, half the cumin, and half the chilli powder in a large bowl;
season with salt and pepper. Roll level tablespoons of mixture into balls.

2 Heat the olive oil in a tagine or large heavy-based pan (see tip) over a
medium heat; cook the meatballs, in two batches, turning, for 5 minutes
or until browned. Remove from the tagine.

3 Cook the onion in the tagine, stirring, for 3 minutes or until softened. Add
the tomato, saffron, and the remaining cumin and chilli; bring to the boil.
Reduce the heat to low; cook for 15 minutes or until the tomatoes soften.

4 Return the meatballs to the tagine; cook for 10 minutes or until the
meatballs are cooked through and the sauce thickens slightly. Season
with salt and pepper to taste. Make four indents in the sauce; carefully
crack the eggs into the indents; cook, covered, for 5 minutes or until
the whites of the eggs are set and the yolks remain runny (or eggs
are cooked to your liking). Sprinkle the tagine with coriander leaves.

TIP

A tagine is both the name of the dish and the
traditional vessel that is used for cooking it in.
It has a flat-bottomed base and a conical lid,
designed to trap the steam and keep the food
moist. An enamelled cast-iron pan that holds
the heat evenly is a good alternative.

Sauces

Many one-pot dishes can benefit from a sauce to be served as a topping or on the side. A fragrant or cooling sauce can make all the difference to a meal, potentially transforming it from a simple supper into a showstopping dinner party dish.

Salsa verde

VEGAN | PREP + COOK TIME **5 MINUTES** | MAKES **$^2/_3$ CUP**

Process or blend 2 cups (40g) firmly packed fresh flat-leaf parsley leaves, 1$^1/_2$ tablespoons of loosely packed fresh lemon thyme leaves, 1 tablespoon of capers, 1 crushed garlic clove, 1 teaspoon of caster sugar, $^1/_2$ cup (60ml) olive oil, and 1$^1/_2$ tablespoons of white wine vinegar until combined. Season with salt and pepper.

Mango chutney yogurt

VEGETARIAN | PREP TIME **5 MINUTES** | MAKES **1$^1/_4$ CUPS**

Combine 1 cup (280g) Greek-style yogurt and 2 teaspoons of lemon juice in a small bowl; season with salt and pepper to taste. Swirl through 2 tablespoons of store-bought mango chutney. Season with freshly ground black pepper.

Raita

VEGETARIAN | PREP + COOK TIME **5 MINUTES + REFRIGERATION AND STANDING** | MAKES **1$^3/_4$ CUPS**

Place a fine sieve over a bowl, spoon in 500g Greek-style yogurt and $^1/_2$ teaspoon of salt. Cover, refrigerate for 2 hours until thicker; discard the liquid. Combine 1 peeled, coarsely grated cucumber and $^1/_2$ teaspoon of salt; stand for 20 minutes. Squeeze out any excess liquid. Combine the yogurt, cucumber, 1 crushed garlic clove and 2 tablespoons of chopped fresh mint leaves. Season with salt and pepper to taste.

Harissa yogurt

VEGETARIAN | PREP + COOK TIME **5 MINUTES** | MAKES **1 CUP**

Combine 1 cup (280g) Greek-style yogurt and 1 teaspoon of honey in a small bowl; season with salt and pepper to taste. Swirl through 2 teaspoons of harissa paste; serve sprinkled with $^1/_2$ teaspoon of ground cumin.

One pot spaghetti marinara

PESCATARIAN | PREP + COOK TIME **25 MINUTES** | SERVES **4**

This dish is so simple, requiring very little preparation. For a vegetarian option, instead of the marinara mix try adding some char-grilled aubergine or marinated antipasto vegetables and fresh rocket at the end of step two.

1 tbsp olive oil

1 medium onion (150g), finely chopped

2 garlic cloves, crushed

1 fresh long red chilli, finely chopped

400g can chopped tomatoes

$1/3$ cup (7g) coarsely chopped fresh basil

1 litre (4 cups) water

500g spaghetti

500g marinara (seafood) mix (see tip)

salt and freshly ground black pepper

2 tbsp olive oil, extra

$1/3$ cup (7g) small fresh basil leaves

1   Heat the olive oil in a large saucepan; cook the onion, garlic, and chilli, stirring, until the onion softens. Add the tomatoes and chopped basil; cook, stirring, for 1 minute.

2   Add the water to the pan; bring to the boil. Add the pasta; once the pasta begins to soften, gently stir it into the tomato mixture. Boil, stirring, for 5 minutes. Add the marinara mix; boil, stirring, for 5 minutes or until the pasta is tender and the seafood is just cooked. Season with salt and pepper to taste.

3   Serve the bowls of pasta drizzled with the extra olive oil and sprinkled with basil leaves.

TIP

This recipe is quite versatile – you could easily change this basic sauce recipe to suit your tastes and needs. You could use the same amount of shelled uncooked prawns, or shredded barbecued chicken, instead of the marinara (seafood) mix.

Cauliflower, capsicum, and chickpea curry

VEGAN | PREP + COOK TIME **40 MINUTES** | SERVES **4**

This curry is so simple to make and packs a punch when it comes to flavour. It also scores high in the nutritional stakes thanks to handfuls of fresh vegetables and chickpeas, high in plant-based protein. Serve with steamed jasmine rice.

2 tbsp olive oil

1 medium onion (150g), thickly sliced

1 large red capsicum (pepper) (350g), thickly sliced

1 garlic clove, crushed

2 tsp finely grated fresh ginger

2 small fresh red Thai chillies, finely chopped

1 tsp ground cumin

1/2 tsp ground turmeric

1/4 tsp ground cardamom

1/4 tsp ground fennel

1 small cauliflower (1kg), trimmed, thickly sliced

400g can chopped tomatoes

400ml can coconut cream

1 cup (250ml) vegetable stock

1 tbsp tomato paste

175g chopped green kale

400g can chickpeas, drained, rinsed

1/2 cup (4g) loosely packed small fresh mint leaves

1 Heat the olive oil in a large saucepan over a medium-high heat; cook the onion, capsicum, garlic, ginger, and chilli, stirring, for 5 minutes or until the onion softens. Add the spices and cauliflower; cook, stirring, for another 2 minutes.

2 Add the tomatoes, coconut cream, stock, and tomato paste; bring to the boil. Reduce the heat; simmer for 20 minutes. Add the kale and chickpeas; simmer for 10 minutes or until the vegetables are tender. Season with salt and pepper to taste.

3 Serve the bowls of curry sprinkled with mint leaves.

One-hour braised chicken with sweet potato

PREP + COOK TIME **1 HOUR** | SERVES **4**

This classic chicken casserole is perfect for a midweek family supper as it's so simple
to make, requiring very little preparation (or washing up!), and results in succulent pieces
of chicken that melt in the mouth.

2 tbsp olive oil

4 x 350g chicken marylands (legs)

2 large red onions (600g), cut into wedges

2 medium sweet potatoes (800g), thickly sliced

1 cup (250ml) chicken stock

2 tsp cornflour

2 tsp water

4 sprigs fresh lemon thyme, plus extra to serve

salt and freshly ground black pepper

1 Preheat oven to 180°C (160°C fan/350°F/Gas 4).

2 Heat the olive oil in a 12-cup (3-litre) casserole or flameproof dish over
a medium heat; cook the chicken, skin-side down, for 5 minutes or until
lightly browned. Turn over; arrange the onion and sweet potato around
the chicken. Pour in the stock, then the combined cornflour and water;
bring to the boil. Add the thyme, season with salt and pepper.

3 Cover the dish, transfer to the oven; cook for 40 minutes or until the
chicken is cooked through and the vegetables are tender. Serve topped
with the extra thyme sprigs.

TIP

You can use chicken thigh cutlets or drumsticks
in this recipe instead of chicken marylands (legs).

Fast lamb and rosemary ragout

PREP + COOK TIME **40 MINUTES** | SERVES **6**

Rich and meaty, this full-flavoured ragout is the ultimate comfort food. Here we've stirred through orecchiette, but you could also serve it topped on any pasta of your choice for a hearty meal that's worth hurrying home for.

2 tbsp olive oil

500g lamb leg steaks or backstraps (eye of loin), cut into 1.5cm pieces

1 medium onion (150g), finely chopped

1 small carrot (70g), coarsely grated

3 garlic cloves, finely chopped

4 anchovy fillets, finely chopped (see tip)

1 tbsp finely chopped fresh rosemary

1/4 cup (60ml) balsamic vinegar

2 tbsp tomato paste

2 x 400g can chopped tomatoes

2 tsp brown sugar

salt and freshly ground black pepper

250g frozen broad beans, thawed, peeled

500g cooked orecchiette pasta

1/2 cup (40g) finely grated parmesan

1/4 cup (5g) fresh basil leaves

1 Heat 1 tablespoon of the olive oil in a large heavy-based saucepan over a high heat; cook the lamb, in batches, for 5 minutes or until browned. Transfer to a bowl; cover to keep warm.

2 Heat another tablespoon of the olive oil in the same pan. Add the onion, carrot, garlic, anchovy, and rosemary; cook, stirring, for 5 minutes or until the onion and carrot soften. Add the vinegar; cook, stirring, for 30 seconds or until evaporated. Add the tomato paste; cook, stirring, for 1 minute or until fragrant.

3 Return the lamb to the pan with the tomatoes and sugar, season with salt and pepper; bring to the boil. Reduce the heat to low; cook, covered, for 10 minutes. Add the broad beans for the last 5 minutes of cooking time.

4 Add the pasta to the lamb ragout; add a splash of water if required and stir over a medium heat until combined. Season with salt and pepper. Serve topped with the parmesan and basil leaves.

TIP

You can omit the anchovies, if preferred, but they do dissolve and bring a savoury complexity to dishes such as this, and are not in any way overpowering.

Balsamic tomato and mushroom chicken

PREP + COOK TIME **25 MINUTES** | SERVES **4**

Golden chicken thighs are married with Mediterranean flavours in this super easy
and nutritious dish that makes a great midweek meal. Serve with crusty bread or
mashed potatoes, if you like.

2 tbsp olive oil

8 x 125g chicken thighs

2 garlic cloves, sliced

8 sprigs fresh thyme

4 flat mushrooms (320g), sliced

250g cherry tomatoes

1 tbsp balsamic vinegar

80g feta, crumbled

1/4 cup (5g) coarsely chopped fresh flat-leaf parsley

1 Heat the olive oil in a large, heavy-based pan over a high heat. Cook the chicken, in batches, for 2 minutes each side or until browned. Remove from the pan.

2 Reduce the heat to medium. Cook the garlic, thyme, and mushrooms, stirring occasionally, for 5 minutes or until browned. Add the tomatoes to the pan; cook, stirring, for 1 minute. Return the chicken to the pan; cook, covered, for 10 minutes or until cooked through.

3 Drizzle the chicken with the balsamic vinegar; sprinkle with the feta and parsley.

Rigatoni with aubergine and Italian sausage

PREP + COOK TIME **30 MINUTES** | SERVES **4**

This family-friendly sausage ragu brings a taste of Italy to your table. Perfect for a weekday supper or for a hearty weekend lunch, everyone will enjoy this flavour-packed pasta dish. Serve with a green salad on the side, if you like.

6 Italian-style pork and fennel sausages (720g)

$\frac{1}{4}$ cup (60ml) olive oil

1 medium onion (150g), finely chopped

2 stalks celery (300g), trimmed, finely chopped

1 garlic clove, crushed

2 tbsp brandy (optional)

1 medium aubergine (300g), chopped

2$\frac{1}{3}$ cups (600g) bottled tomato passata

$\frac{1}{2}$ cup (140g) tomato paste

$\frac{1}{2}$ cup (125ml) water

salt and freshly ground black pepper

375g rigatoni pasta

2 tbsp fresh basil leaves

$\frac{1}{4}$ cup (20g) shaved parmesan

1 Squeeze the sausage meat from the casings into a medium bowl; discard the casings. Coarsely crumble the sausage meat.

2 Heat a large saucepan over a high heat; cook the sausage meat, stirring, for 8 minutes or until browned. Remove from the pan; drain on paper towel.

3 Add the olive oil to the same pan; reduce the heat to medium-high. Cook the onion, celery, and garlic, stirring, for 5 minutes or until the onion softens. Add the brandy, if using; cook, stirring, until the brandy evaporates. Add the aubergine; cook, stirring, until tender.

4 Return the sausage meat to the pan with the passata, tomato paste, and water; bring to the boil. Reduce the heat; simmer for 10 minutes or until the sauce thickens slightly. Season with salt and pepper to taste.

5 Meanwhile, cook the pasta in a large saucepan of boiling salted water until tender; drain. Return to the pan to keep warm.

6 Add the sauce to the pasta in the pan; toss to combine. Serve topped with the basil and parmesan.

Spanish chicken and chorizo stew

PREP + COOK TIME **40 MINUTES** | SERVES **6**

So easy to prepare and bursting with Spanish flavours this smoky, rich, and hearty stew will become a go-to weekday meal as you realise how simple it is to bring a taste of sunny Spain to your table. Accompany with crusty bread rolls, if you like.

1 cup (250ml) chicken stock

pinch saffron threads

340g cured chorizo sausage, thickly sliced

1.5kg chicken drumsticks

2 tsp olive oil

1 medium onion (150g), thickly sliced

1 medium red capsicum (pepper) (200g), thickly sliced

2 tsp smoked paprika

2 x 400g can chopped tomatoes

$^1/_2$ cup (60g) pitted black olives

$^1/_4$ cup (15g) fresh flat-leaf parsley leaves

1 Combine the stock and saffron in a bowl. Reserve until required.

2 Cook the chorizo in a large saucepan, over a medium heat, until browned on both sides. Drain on paper towel.

3 Cook the chicken, in batches, in the same pan, for about 3 minutes each side, or until browned all over. Remove from the pan.

4 Heat the olive oil in the same pan; cook the onion and capsicum, stirring, for 2 minutes or until the onion softens. Add the paprika; cook, stirring, until fragrant.

5 Return the chorizo and chicken to the pan. Add the stock mixture and tomatoes, cover; bring to the boil. Reduce the heat; simmer, covered, for 20 minutes or until the chicken is cooked through. Stir in the olives.

6 Serve the stew sprinkled with parsley.

Super-green vegetable curry

VEGAN | PREP + COOK TIME **55 MINUTES** | SERVES **4**

Fresh and fragrant this delicious Thai-inspired green curry is full of flavour and packed
with nutritious greens. Serve accompanied with steamed basmati rice and topped
with toasted flaked coconut.

½ cup (125ml) grapeseed oil

4 garlic cloves, peeled

1 cup (20g) fresh basil leaves

5cm piece fresh ginger, finely chopped

1 fresh long green chilli, seeded, thinly sliced

1 bunch fresh coriander, stalks and roots reserved

200g kale, washed, sliced

120g baby spinach leaves

600g baby aubergines, cut
into 1.5cm slices

670ml canned coconut milk, shaken well

2 cups (500ml) vegetable stock

1 cup (200g) pearl barley, rinsed

150g green beans

1 cup (120g) frozen peas, thawed

150g sugar snap peas

salt and freshly ground black pepper

lime wedges, to serve

1 Process half the oil, the garlic, basil, ginger, chilli, coriander stalks
and roots, half the kale, and half the spinach until a smooth paste
forms; reserve ¼ cup (75g) curry paste.

2 Heat the remaining oil in a large heavy-based saucepan over a high
heat; cook the aubergine, in batches, for 3 minutes on each side or
until golden and softened. Drain on paper towel.

3 Reduce the heat to medium, add the green curry paste; cook, stirring,
for 1 minute or until fragrant. Add the coconut milk, stock, and pearl
barley; stir to combine. Cook, covered, for 20 minutes or until the pearl
barley is just tender.

4 Stir in the green beans, peas, sugar snap peas, remaining kale, and the
remaining spinach; cook for 3 minutes or until the beans are just tender
and the pearl barley is soft.

5 Top with coriander leaves, season with salt and pepper to taste.
Serve with lime wedges.

TIP

Wash the coriander thoroughly, as the roots and
stems can sometimes be very sandy.

Bread sides

One pot dishes are often well suited to a bread side, whether it's for mopping up all that delicious sauce in stews, casseroles, and tagines, dipping in soups, or to provide a neutral counterpoint to curries and other spicy dishes.

Garlic naan

VEGAN | PREP + COOK TIME **25 MINUTES** | MAKES **4**

Preheat oven to 180°C (160°C fan/350°F/Gas 4). Place 4 plain naan breads on a baking-paper-lined oven tray; prick all over with a fork. Combine 1/3 cup (40ml) extra virgin olive oil, 2 crushed garlic cloves, and 2 tablespoons of coarsely chopped fresh chives or coriander in a small bowl; season with salt and pepper. Spread the herb and garlic mixture evenly on the bread. Bake for 15 minutes or until the bread is golden and crisp.

Simple yogurt flatbread

VEGETARIAN | PREP + COOK TIME **20 MINUTES + STANDING** | MAKES **4**

Place 1 cup (150g) self-raising flour in a medium bowl; cut in 1/2 cup (140g) Greek-style yogurt with a butter knife. Bring the mixture together with your hands. Knead the dough lightly until smooth. Stand for 5 minutes. Divide the dough into four pieces; roll each piece on a floured surface to about a 20cm long oval. Heat 2 teaspoons of olive oil in a medium frying pan over a high heat. Cook one piece of dough at a time for 30 seconds on each side, or until puffy and golden, adding extra oil to the pan each time. Scatter with flat-leaf parsley leaves, if you like.

Grilled sourdough

VEGAN | PREP + COOK TIME **10 MINUTES** | SERVES **4**

Cut 8 thin slices from a loaf of sourdough bread. Brush the bread lightly with extra virgin olive oil; place on a heated oiled grill plate (or grill or barbecue) for 1 minute on each side or until lightly charred. Rub with a cut garlic clove, if you like.

Cheddar toasts

VEGETARIAN | PREP TIME **15 MINUTES** | SERVES **4**

Preheat oven to 200°C (180°C fan/400°F/Gas 6). Place 8 slices of sourdough on a baking-paper-lined oven tray; top with 150g sliced cheddar. Bake for 8 minutes or until the cheddar melts. Sprinkle with freshly ground black pepper, if you like.

Cheat's dhal with curry sprinkles

VEGETARIAN | PREP + COOK TIME **25 MINUTES + STANDING** | SERVES **4**

Traditionally dhal is cooked long and slow, but this tasty twist on one of India's staple dishes is ready in under half an hour, making it a perfect midweek meal. Serve with naan or pappadums, if you like.

1 tbsp coconut oil or ghee

2 small sweet potatoes (500g), coarsely grated

4 green onions (spring onions), thinly sliced

1 garlic clove, crushed

2 tsp finely grated fresh ginger

2 tsp garam masala

1 tsp brown mustard seeds

400g can brown lentils, drained, rinsed

400g can diced tomatoes

salt and freshly ground black pepper

1 cup (280g) Greek-style yogurt

curry sprinkles

¼ cup (20g) shredded coconut

1 tbsp sunflower seeds

1 tbsp pepitas (pumpkin seeds)

1 tbsp raisins

2 tsp pure maple syrup

2 tbsp fresh curry leaves

½ tsp ground cumin

½ tsp ground turmeric

¼ tsp curry powder

1   To make the curry sprinkles, stir the ingredients in a medium saucepan over a low heat for 4 minutes or until golden. Remove. Set aside.

2   Heat the coconut oil in the same saucepan over a high heat; cook the sweet potato, green onion, garlic, and ginger, stirring, for 3 minutes or until softened. Add the garam masala and mustard seeds; cook, stirring, for 30 seconds or until fragrant.

3   Add the lentils, tomatoes, and ½ cup (125ml) water to the pan; bring to a simmer. Cook, stirring frequently, for 5 minutes or until thick. Mash coarsely. Season with salt and pepper to taste.

4   Serve the dhal topped with the yogurt and curry sprinkles.

Wholemeal spaghetti with mushrooms and almonds

VEGETARIAN | PREP + COOK TIME **35 MINUTES** | SERVES **4**

Crunchy roasted almonds and earthy mushrooms are paired together in this nutritious pasta dish. You can use your favourite variety of mushrooms; button and cap mushrooms will work well.

375g wholegrain spaghetti

2 tbsp olive oil

400g Swiss brown mushrooms, sliced

400g portobello mushrooms, sliced

2 shallots (50g), coarsely chopped

2 cloves garlic, coarsely chopped

salt and freshly ground black pepper

1/2 cup (80g) coarsely chopped roasted almonds

150g baby spinach leaves

1/2 cup (40g) finely grated pecorino cheese

1/4 cup (15g) fresh flat-leaf parsley leaves

1 Cook the pasta in a large saucepan of boiling salted water until just tender; drain, reserving 1 cup (250ml) of the cooking liquid. Remove the pasta from the pan; set aside and cover to keep warm.

2 Add the olive oil to the same pan over a high heat; cook the mushrooms and shallots, stirring occasionally, for 5 minutes or until the mushrooms are lightly golden and the shallots are tender (see tip). Add the garlic; cook, stirring, for about 1 minute or until fragrant. Season with salt and pepper to taste.

3 Reduce the heat to low; toss the warm pasta, almonds, and spinach through the mushroom mixture. Add enough reserved pasta water to lightly coat the pasta. Serve topped with the cheese and parsley.

Bacon, cider, and fennel mussels

PREP + COOK TIME **15 MINUTES** | SERVES **2**

Fresh, flavoursome, and so quick to make, this one-pot dish will become a firm favourite.
Serve these mussels steamed in cider with plenty of crusty bread to mop up the
cooking juices, or Belgian style, with thin chips and mayonnaise.

1 tbsp olive oil

1 rindless bacon slice (80g), chopped

2 garlic cloves, thinly sliced

1 baby fennel bulb (130g), thinly sliced, fronds reserved

1kg pot-ready mussels (see tip)

³/₄ cup (180ml) dry cider

1 Heat the olive oil in a large saucepan over a medium heat. Cook the bacon, garlic, and fennel, stirring, for 3 minutes or until browned.

2 Add the mussels and cider to the pan; bring to the boil. Cover the pan with a lid; cook, shaking the pan occasionally, for about 5 minutes or until the mussels start to open.

3 Serve the mussels topped with the reserved fennel fronds, and accompanied with bread.

TIP

Pot-ready or pre-bagged mussels are generally sold cleaned and ready to use. If you have bought loose mussels, scrub the shells to remove the debris, then remove the beard – the hair-like byssal thread – by yanking it down.

Seafood risoni paella

PREP + COOK TIME **1 HOUR** | SERVES **4**

In this twist on the classic Spanish dish of paella we've used risoni pasta instead of rice, creating a wonderful textured base that showcases the seafood at its best. A great communal meal, serve the paella straight from the pan at your table.

2 tbsp olive oil

1 small onion (80g), finely chopped

4 garlic cloves, crushed

500g risoni pasta

pinch saffron threads

1 cup (250ml) dry white wine

6 small tomatoes (540g), seeded, coarsely chopped

2 tbsp tomato paste

1 tsp finely grated orange rind

4 sprigs fresh marjoram

4 cups (1 litre) chicken stock, warmed

salt and freshly ground black pepper

1½ cups (180g) frozen peas

⅓ cup (80g) finely chopped drained char-grilled capsicum (pepper)

500g pot-ready mussels (see tips)

4 large uncooked king prawns (280g), peeled, deveined, leaving heads and tails intact

1 large cleaned squid hood (150g), cut into 1cm thick rings

⅓ cup (6g) coarsely chopped fresh flat-leaf parsley

lemon wedges, to serve

1 Heat the olive oil in a paella pan (see tips) over a medium-high heat; cook the onion and garlic, stirring, for 5 minutes or until the onion softens. Add the pasta and saffron; stir to coat in the onion mixture. Stir in the wine, tomatoes, tomato paste, orange rind, and marjoram; cook, stirring, until the wine has almost evaporated.

2 Add 1 cup (250ml) of the stock; stir until the liquid is absorbed. Add the remaining stock; cook, stirring, for 8 minutes or until the pasta is almost tender. Season with salt and pepper to taste.

3 Place the peas, capsicum, and seafood on top of the risoni mixture; do not stir to combine. Cover the pan, reduce the heat; simmer for 10 minutes or until the seafood has changed colour and the mussels have opened. Sprinkle with parsley; serve with lemon wedges.

TIPS

- You can use 750g uncooked marinara seafood mix instead of the mussels, prawns, and squid.
- This recipe can be made in a traditional paella pan if you own one, otherwise a heavy-based saucepan, deep frying pan, or wok with a tight-fitting lid will work just as well.

Hot and sour chicken noodle soup

PREP + COOK TIME **25 MINUTES** | SERVES **4**

This bold, fragrant chicken noodle soup is known as Tom Yum in Thailand. The word *tom* relates to boiling while *yum* refers to the distinctive spicy and sour flavour combination. Not only delicious, it is said to have both immune-boosting and anti-inflammatory properties.

1½ cups (375ml) chicken stock

1.5 litres (6 cups) water

3 fresh makrut lime leaves, torn in half

10cm stick fresh lemongrass (20g), halved lengthways

3cm piece fresh ginger (15g), thinly sliced

⅓ cup (100g) tom yum paste

2 tbsp fish sauce

½ cup (125ml) lime juice

⅓ cup (75g) firmly packed brown sugar

200g dried rice stick noodles

salt and freshly ground black pepper

400g baby bok choy (pak choi), quartered

200g fresh shiitake mushrooms, thinly sliced

400g chicken breast fillets, thinly sliced

3 small fresh red Thai chillies, thinly sliced

¼ cup (4g) fresh coriander leaves

1 Place the stock, water, lime leaves, lemongrass, and ginger in a large saucepan; bring to the boil. Reduce the heat; simmer, covered, for 5 minutes. Remove the lemongrass and ginger with a slotted spoon. Stir in the tom yum paste; return to the boil. Stir in the fish sauce, lime juice, and sugar.

2 Meanwhile, place the noodles in a large heatproof bowl; cover with boiling water, stand for 5 minutes or until tender. Drain.

3 Add the bok choy to the stock mixture with the mushrooms, chicken, and two of the sliced chillies; simmer until the chicken is cooked through. Stir in the noodles; simmer until hot. Season with salt and pepper.

4 Serve soup topped with remaining chilli, coriander, and a squeeze of lime, if you like.

TIP

To save time, you can use chicken stir-fry strips instead of the breast fillet.

Korean beef ribs with kimchi

PREP + COOK TIME **2 HOURS 30 MINUTES** | SERVES **8**

Spicy, fragrant, and cooked to perfection until the beef is tender and falls from the bone, this classic Korean dish boasts an umami depth, with slightly sweet overtones. Delicious with kimchi, a Korean speciality side dish comprising of fermented cabbage and radish.

2kg beef short ribs, cut into 6cm lengths

salt and freshly ground black pepper

1 tbsp peanut oil

1 bunch green onions (spring onions)

1¹/₂ tbsp finely chopped fresh ginger

3 garlic cloves, crushed

1¹/₂ tbsp sesame oil

2 tbsp rice wine vinegar

2 tbsp soy sauce

1¹/₂ tbsp gochujang (see tips)

1 cup (100g) kimchi

1 medium firm pear (230g), coarsely grated

200g fresh shiitake mushrooms

500g baby bok choy (pak choi), quartered lengthways

200g enoki mushrooms

sesame seeds and gochugaru (see tips), to serve (optional)

1 Season the ribs with salt and pepper. Heat the oil in a large heavy-based saucepan or flameproof casserole dish over a high heat. Cook the ribs, in batches, turning occasionally, for 8 minutes or until browned all over; transfer each batch to a large heatproof bowl.

2 Chop the white part of the green onions; refrigerate the green tops, reserve for serving. Add the white part of the onion to the pan with the ginger and garlic; cook, stirring, for 30 seconds or until fragrant.

3 Whisk the sesame oil, rice wine vinegar, soy sauce, and gochujang in a large jug until combined. Add the mixture to the pan with the kimchi, pear, and 6 cups (1.5 litres) of water; bring to a simmer. Reduce the heat to low; cook, covered, stirring every 30 minutes, for 1¹/₂ hours. Add the shiitake mushrooms; cook for a further 30 minutes or until the beef is tender and falls away from the bone.

4 Place the bok choy and enoki mushrooms on top of the beef rib mixture in the pan. Cook, covered, for a further 2 minutes or until the vegetables are just tender.

5 Trim the reserved green onion tops; cut into long thin strips. Serve half the beef rib mixture with all the bok choy, topped with green onion strips, sesame seeds, and gochugaru if using. Transfer the remaining beef rib mixture to an airtight container; cool, then store.

TIPS

- Gochujang is a Korean chilli paste available from Asian food stores. We used a mild gochujang paste; you can use hot if preferred.
- Gochugaru are Korean chilli flakes, available in jars from Asian food stores.

Spicy aubergine with soft-boiled eggs and labneh

VEGETARIAN | PREP + COOK TIME **30 MINUTES** | SERVES **4**

This is a traditional Middle Eastern dish known as shakshuka, often eaten for breakfast but delicious served at any time of day. A hearty and chunky tomato and aubergine-based sauce serves as a bed for perfectly cooked soft-boiled eggs.

8 eggs

2 tbsp extra virgin olive oil

1 large aubergine (500g), cut into 2.5cm pieces

1 large onion (200g), chopped

1 fresh long red chilli, thinly sliced

2 garlic cloves, crushed

2 tsp ground cumin

1 tsp ground coriander

400g can chickpeas, drained, rinsed

2 x 400g can chopped tomatoes

1 cup (250ml) vegetable stock

salt and freshly ground black pepper

160g drained labneh

80g baby spinach leaves

$1/2$ teaspoon sumac

Turkish bread (430g), toasted, to serve

1 Place the eggs in a large saucepan; cover with cold water. Put a lid on the pan; bring to the boil. Boil the eggs, uncovered, for 2 minutes. Drain immediately. Place the eggs in a bowl of cold water to cool.

2 Heat half the olive oil in the saucepan over a high heat; cook the aubergine, stirring, until browned and tender. Remove from the pan. Heat the remaining oil in the same pan; cook the onion and chilli, stirring, until soft and lightly browned. Add the garlic, cumin, and coriander; cook, stirring, until fragrant.

3 Return the aubergine to the pan with the chickpeas, tomatoes, and stock; simmer, covered, for 15 minutes. Season with salt and pepper to taste.

4 Meanwhile, carefully peel the eggs.

5 Divide the aubergine mixture between 4 shallow serving bowls; top with the halved eggs, labneh, and spinach leaves. Sprinkle with sumac; serve with lightly toasted Turkish bread.

TIP

To get a perfectly centred yolk in boiled eggs, gently stir the eggs with a wooden spoon until the water comes to the boil.

FRYING PAN

These dishes come straight out of the frying pan and onto a plate. With minimum fuss and washing up, you can whip up anything from frittatas and quesadillas to pies and pilaf.

Egg and sausage bake

PREP + COOK TIME **20 MINUTES** | SERVES **1**

Try pork and fennel sausages or even a spicy sausage, like fresh chorizo or merguez, for added flavour. You need an ovenproof frying pan for this recipe; if you don't have one, wrap the handle of the frying pan with a few layers of foil to protect it from the heat of the oven.

2 pork sausages (240g)

20g butter

2 large flat mushrooms, coarsely chopped

80g baby spinach leaves

6 cherry tomatoes, halved

1 egg

salt and freshly ground black pepper

1 slice sourdough bread, torn into chunks

2 tbsp finely grated parmesan

2 tbsp fresh flat-leaf parsley leaves

1 Preheat oven to 200°C (180°C fan/400°F/Gas 6).

2 Cook the sausages in a small ovenproof frying pan, over a medium heat, for 6 minutes or until just cooked; remove from the pan. Cool slightly, then cut each sausage into chunks.

3 Add the butter and mushroom to the same pan; cook, stirring, for 1 minute or until tender. Add three-quarters of the spinach; stir until just wilted.

4 Return the sausage to the pan; add the tomatoes, then carefully break the egg on top of the tomato. Season with salt and pepper and top with the bread.

5 Transfer the pan to the oven; bake for 8 minutes or until the egg white is set, the yolk is still runny, and the bread is browned. Top with the remaining spinach; sprinkle over the parmesan and parsley.

TIP

You can swap the spinach for rocket or kale, while the bread can be any variety you have on hand.

Malaysian fish curry

PESCATARIAN | PREP + COOK TIME **15 MINUTES** | SERVES **6**

This mild and fragrant fish curry looks impressive, is full of flavour and nutrition, and is so easy to cook. We used Desiree potatoes for this recipe and left the skins on; use any potato you like – baby new potatoes would also work well.

1 tbsp vegetable oil

2 medium potatoes (400g), cut into wedges

500g firm white fish fillets, cut into 2.5cm pieces

1 medium brown onion (150g), thinly sliced

1 garlic clove, crushed

1 cinnamon stick

820g mild Malaysian curry sauce

1/3 cup (45g) roasted peanuts, coarsely chopped

1/2 cup (8g) fresh coriander leaves

1 Heat the oil in a large deep frying pan over a high heat; cook the potatoes, in batches, until browned all over. Remove from the pan. Add the fish to the pan, in batches; cook until browned. Remove from the pan.

2 Cook the onion and garlic in the same pan, stirring, until the onion softens. Return the potatoes to the pan with the cinnamon and curry sauce; bring to the boil. Reduce the heat; simmer, uncovered, for about 5 minutes or until the potato is tender. Add the fish; simmer, uncovered, for 1 minute or until the fish is cooked through.

3 Remove the cinnamon stick from the curry. Top the curry with the peanuts and coriander. Serve with steamed rice and green beans, if you like.

Frying pan beef and spinach lasagne

PREP + COOK TIME **30 MINUTES** | SERVES **6**

This speedy and fuss-free modern take on a lasagne is cooked on the hob then grilled for a golden cheesy topping. Ready in just 30 minutes, it's simple enough to rustle up for a midweek supper. Serve with a mixed-leaf salad and garlic bread on the side, if you like.

1 tbsp olive oil

1 large onion (200g), finely chopped

2 garlic cloves, crushed

375g packet fresh lasagne sheets

60g baby spinach leaves

900g ready-made fresh bolognese pasta sauce with beef

1 cup (250ml) water

1¹/₂ cups (360g) firm ricotta, crumbled

1¹/₂ cups (150g) coarsely grated mozzarella

¹/₃ cup (6g) small fresh basil leaves

1   Heat the olive oil in a large deep frying pan (see tip) over a medium-high heat; cook the onion and garlic, stirring, for 5 minutes or until the onion softens.

2   Meanwhile, tear the lasagne sheets lengthways into strips; put the long strips aside, save any small broken pieces. Sprinkle the small broken pasta pieces and spinach into the pan with the onion; mix gently to combine. Pour the combined pasta sauce and water into the pan; mix gently to combine.

3   Insert the long pasta strips, standing them upright on the long sides, into the mixture. Sprinkle with both cheeses. Bring the pan to the boil over a high heat. Reduce the heat to low; simmer for 2 minutes or until the pasta is tender.

4   Preheat grill.

5   Grill the lasagne for about 5 minutes or until the cheese browns. Cover, stand for 5 minutes before serving. Sprinkle with basil leaves.

TIP

You need a frying pan with an ovenproof handle for this recipe, or cover the handle with a few layers of foil to protect it from the heat of the grill. Alternatively, you could use a large flameproof baking dish (about 12-cups/3-litres) instead of the frying pan, if you prefer.

Red onion tarte tatin with crunchy nut topping

VEGETARIAN | PREP + COOK TIME **1 HOUR 5 MINUTES** | SERVES **4**

Use rolled oats instead of rolled rye in the nut topping, if you like. Draining the liquid from the pan in step 2 helps stop the pastry from becoming soggy, and the reduced pan juices provide a delicious dressing for the salad. The tart is best served right after baking.

2 tbsp olive oil

6 small red onions (600g), halved crossways

4 small fresh thyme sprigs

1 tbsp balsamic vinegar

1 tbsp honey

2 garlic cloves, thinly sliced

salt and freshly ground black pepper

150g ripe tomatoes, thinly sliced

2 sheets frozen puff pastry (330g), thawed

80g soft goat's cheese

2 medium fresh figs (120g), quartered

1 small courgette (90g), thinly sliced lengthways

60g watercress sprigs or baby rocket

crunchy nut topping

2 tbsp pecans, coarsely chopped

2 tbsp rolled rye

2 tbsp pepitas (pumpkin seeds)

1 tsp poppy seeds

olive-oil spray

1 Preheat oven to 200°C (180°C fan/400°F/Gas 6).

2 Heat the olive oil in a 26cm straight-sided, heavy-based oven-proof frying pan over a medium heat. Add the onion, cut-side up, and the thyme; cook for 5 minutes. Add the vinegar and honey; cook for 2 minutes. Turn the onion carefully so that the cut-side faces down and top evenly with the garlic; season with salt and pepper. Bake for 15 minutes or until the onion is softened. Using a lid to keep the vegetables in place, drain the liquid from the pan into a bowl; reserve. Place the tomato slices on top of the onion.

3 Place the puff pastry on a clean work surface; use a rolling pin to join the pastry sheets together. Carefully lay the pastry over the pan; trim the excess, tucking the edges in around the onion and tomato.

4 Bake for 30 minutes or until the pastry is puffed, browned, and cooked through. Leave to cool slightly; turn out carefully onto a large plate or chopping board.

5 Meanwhile, make the crunchy nut topping. Combine the pecans, rolled rye, pepitas, and poppy seeds in the frying pan. Spray lightly with oil; roast for 7 minutes or until light golden and crisp. Season with salt and pepper to taste; remove from the pan and set aside to cool.

6 Add the reserved cooking liquid back to the pan and bring to a simmer; simmer for 5 minutes or until syrupy.

7 Top the tart with the goat's cheese, figs, and crunchy nut topping. Combine the courgette and watercress in a small bowl. Drizzle the tart and salad with the reduced cooking liquid; serve immediately.

Tomato, mozzarella, and chickpea pan bake

VEGETARIAN | PREP + COOK TIME **1 HOUR** | SERVES **6**

Inspired by Italian flavours this delicious cheesy bake is easy to throw together
and perfect for a simple weeknight dinner. Serve with a side of green salad and
crusty garlic bread, if you like.

½ loaf ciabatta (300g), crusts removed, torn into 2cm pieces

400g grape (cherry) tomatoes, halved lengthways

⅓ cup (80ml) extra virgin olive oil

salt and freshly ground black pepper

400g can chickpeas, drained, rinsed

100g fresh ricotta

10 eggs, lightly beaten

2 garlic cloves, crushed

¾ cup coarsely chopped fresh flat-leaf parsley

½ cup (40g) finely grated parmesan
(make sure it doesn't contain animal rennet)

1 tbsp drained, rinsed baby capers

⅔ cup (100g) pitted black olives, halved

1 ball buffalo mozzarella (110g), torn (see tip)

2 tbsp fresh basil leaves, torn

1 Preheat oven to 220°C (200°C fan/425°F/Gas 7).

2 Place the bread in an ovenproof 26cm heavy-based frying pan. Squeeze the seeds and juice from the tomatoes over the bread. Reserve the tomato flesh. Drizzle the bread with half the olive oil; season with salt and pepper. Cook over a medium-high heat, stirring occasionally, for 10 minutes or until the bread is golden. Remove from the pan. Add the tomato flesh to the same pan; cook, stirring occasionally, until the tomatoes are softened. Remove from the pan. Wipe out the pan with paper towel.

3 Meanwhile, using a potato masher, lightly crush the chickpeas in a large bowl; season with salt and pepper. Whisk in the ricotta, eggs, garlic, parsley, and three-quarters of the parmesan until combined. Stir in the capers, olives, half the bread, and half the tomatoes; season with salt and pepper.

4 Heat the remaining olive oil in the same pan over a medium heat until hot. Add the egg mixture; top with the remaining bread, tomatoes, and parmesan. Cook for 8 minutes or until browned around the edge and half-set.

5 Cover loosely with baking paper; bake in the oven for 15 minutes or until set. Stand for 5 minutes. Invert onto a large plate. Flip onto a second large plate right-way up.

6 Top with the mozzarella and basil. Serve drizzled with a little extra oil.

TIP

Buffalo mozzarella has a more tangy lactic dairy taste than cow's milk mozzarella. You can use bocconcini instead, if you prefer.

Mashes

Mash makes a perfect side to many one-pot dishes, great for providing a contrasting texture and flavour counterpoint. Try a classic buttery mash or mix it up with added ingredients. Floury and all-rounder potatoes are best for mash; try King Edward, Maris Piper, or Desiree.

Basic potato mash

VEGETARIAN | PREP + COOK TIME **30 MINUTES** | SERVES **4**

Place 1kg peeled, coarsely chopped potatoes in a medium saucepan with enough cold water to barely cover them. Boil, over a medium heat, for 15 minutes or until the potato is tender; drain. Return the potato to the pan, mash until smooth (or use a potato ricer or mouli). Add 40g butter and $^3/_4$ cup (180ml) hot milk; fold in gently until the mash is smooth. Season with salt and pepper to taste.

Mustard and cheddar mash

VEGETARIAN | PREP + COOK TIME **30 MINUTES** | SERVES **4**

Make the basic potato mash (above). When adding the butter and milk, also add 2 tablespoons of Dijon or wholegrain mustard and 1 cup (120g) grated vintage cheddar. Return the pan to the heat; stir the mash over a medium heat until smooth and the cheese melts. Season with salt and pepper to taste. Serve topped with extra grated vintage cheddar.

Kale mash

VEGETARIAN | PREP + COOK TIME **30 MINUTES** | SERVES **4**

Boil 1kg potatoes as directed for the basic potato mash (left); drain. Wipe the pan dry. Heat $^1/_3$ cup (80ml) olive oil in pan; cook 125g shredded kale and 1 chopped garlic clove, stirring, over a medium heat for 5 minutes until the kale wilts. Remove from the pan. Return the potatoes to the pan with 30g butter and $^3/_4$ cup (180ml) hot milk; mash until smooth. Stir in the kale; season with salt and pepper to taste.

Olive oil and sage mash

VEGETARIAN | PREP + COOK TIME **30 MINUTES** | SERVES **4**

Boil 1kg potatoes as directed for basic potato mash (left); drain. Wipe the pan dry. Heat $^1/_3$ cup (80ml) olive oil in the same pan; fry 2 thinly sliced garlic cloves and 2 tablespoons of sage leaves until crisp. Remove with a slotted spoon. Return the potatoes to the pan with ½ cup (120ml) hot milk; mash until smooth. Season with salt and pepper to taste. Serve topped with the garlic and sage.

Chicken with pancetta and white beans

PREP + COOK TIME **35 MINUTES** | SERVES **4**

Pancetta is an Italian unsmoked bacon prepared from pork belly, cured in salt and spices,
then rolled into a sausage shape and dried for several weeks. When cooking with pancetta,
a little goes a long way. Serve this dish with a rocket salad, if you like.

4 chicken thigh cutlets, skin on (800g)

2 tbsp fresh thyme leaves

salt and freshly ground black pepper

1 tbsp olive oil

8 pickling onions (320g)

2 garlic cloves, thinly sliced

100g thinly sliced pancetta

2 drained anchovy fillets

1/4 cup (60ml) dry red wine

400g can white beans, drained, rinsed

salt and freshly ground black pepper

1/3 cup (25g) finely grated parmesan

1 Using a small sharp knife, cut two 2.5cm slits into each chicken
   cutlet; fill the cuts with half the thyme. Season the chicken with salt
   and pepper.

2 Heat the olive oil in a large deep frying pan; cook the chicken, skin-side
   down, for 5 minutes or until lightly browned.

3 Meanwhile, peel the onions, leaving the root ends intact; quarter the
   onions. Turn the chicken and add the onion to the pan; cook, covered,
   for 5 minutes or until the onion is soft and lightly browned.

4 Add the garlic to the pan with the pancetta, anchovies, and remaining
   thyme; cook, stirring, until the pancetta is crisp. Add the wine and beans;
   bring to the boil. Reduce the heat; simmer, uncovered, for 5 minutes or
   until the chicken is cooked. Season with salt and pepper to taste.

5 Serve sprinkled with parmesan.

Prawn and veg Japanese pancake

PREP + COOK TIME **25 MINUTES** | SERVES **1**

Japanese pancakes, or okonomiyaki as they are also known – meaning "what you like" – are customized using a variety of toppings for texture and flavour. You could also add prepared fried noodles and shredded nori, or even pickled pink ginger, to this pancake, if you like.

1 tbsp tomato sauce (ketchup)

2^1/$_2$ tsp Worcestershire sauce

1^1/$_2$ tsp oyster sauce

1 tsp caster sugar

^{1}/$_4$ cup (35g) plain flour

^{1}/$_4$ cup (60ml) water

1 egg

4 uncooked small king prawns (100g), shelled, coarsely chopped

1 small courgette (90g), coarsely grated

1 baby carrot (20g), coarsely grated

1 cup (80g) thinly sliced cabbage

3 green onions (spring onions), thinly sliced

salt and freshly ground black pepper

2 tsp vegetable oil

2 slices streaky bacon (60g), trimmed to fit pan

Japanese-style mayonnaise (Kewpie) and lemon cheek, to serve

1   Preheat grill to a high heat.

2   Whisk the tomato sauce, Worcestershire sauce, oyster sauce, and sugar in a small bowl.

3   Whisk the flour, water, and egg in a medium bowl until smooth. Add the prawn, courgette, carrot, half the cabbage, and half the green onion to the egg mixture; season with salt and pepper.

4   Heat the oil in a 16cm ovenproof frying pan (see tips) over a medium-high heat. Add the pancake mixture; spread evenly in the pan. Cook for 4 minutes or until golden on the bottom. Place the bacon over the top; transfer to the grill. Cook for 8 minutes or until golden and cooked through.

5   Slide the pancake onto a plate. Drizzle with the sauce mixture and mayonnaise; sprinkle with the remaining onion and cabbage; serve with a lemon cheek.

TIPS

- If your frying pan is a few centimetres smaller or larger, simply adjust the cooking time slightly to compensate for the different thickness of the pancake.
- If you don't have an ovenproof frying pan, wrap the handle with a few layers of foil to protect it from the heat of the grill.

Chilli con carne cornbread pie

PREP + COOK TIME **1 HOUR** | SERVES **6**

This twist on a chilli con carne is topped with a crunchy cornbread crust. To make this dish vegetarian, omit the beef and replace with another two cans of four-bean mix. Sprinkle with small fresh flat-leaf parsley sprigs before serving, if you like.

1 tbsp olive oil

1 medium onion (150g), thinly sliced

1 medium red capsicum (pepper) (200g), seeded, thinly sliced

2 garlic cloves, crushed

2 tsp Mexican chilli powder or sweet paprika

2 tsp ground cumin

1 tsp dried rigani (Greek oregano)

750g minced beef

2 x 400g can chopped tomatoes

1 cup (250ml) vegetable stock

2 x 400g can four-bean mix, drained, rinsed

salt and freshly ground black pepper

³/₄ cup (110g) self-raising flour

³/₄ cup (125g) polenta

90g butter, coarsely chopped

1 egg, lightly beaten

¹/₃ cup (40g) coarsely grated cheddar

125g canned corn kernels (sweetcorn), drained

2 tbsp milk, approximately

tomato and avocado salad

1 medium avocado (240g), thinly sliced

400g mixed cherry tomatoes

¹/₃ cup (5g) fresh coriander leaves

¹/₂ small red onion (50g), halved lengthways, thinly sliced

2 tbsp lime juice

1 Heat the olive oil in a large heavy-based saucepan over a medium-high heat; cook the onion, capsicum, and garlic, stirring, for 5 minutes or until the onion softens. Add the chilli, cumin, and oregano; cook, stirring, for 1 minute or until fragrant. Add the beef; cook, stirring, using a wooden spoon to break up any clumps, for 5 minutes or until browned. Add the tomatoes, stock, and bean mix; bring to the boil. Reduce the heat to low-medium; simmer for 20 minutes or until the sauce thickens slightly. Season with salt and pepper to taste.

2 Meanwhile, preheat oven to 200°C (180°C fan/400°F/Gas 6). Place the flour and polenta in a medium bowl; rub in the butter. Stir in the egg, cheddar, half the sweetcorn, and enough milk to make a soft, sticky dough.

3 Spoon the beef mixture into an 8-cup (2-litre) ovenproof frying pan or ovenproof dish. Drop tablespoons of the cornbread dough on top of the beef mixture; top with the remaining sweetcorn. Bake for 20 minutes or until browned.

4 Meanwhile, make the tomato and avocado salad. Combine the ingredients gently in a small bowl; season with salt and pepper.

5 Serve the cornbread pie with the salad.

Chicken and thyme one-pan pie

PREP + COOK TIME **1 HOUR + COOLING** | SERVES **4**

This golden flaky pastry topped chicken pie is classic comfort food, perfect for a warming dinner on a chilly winter's night. Serve with steamed broccoli or any other steamed green vegetables of your choice.

800g chicken thigh fillets, thinly sliced

salt and freshly ground black pepper

2 tbsp olive oil

1 large leek (500g), thinly sliced

2 garlic cloves, crushed

1 tbsp fresh thyme leaves, plus extra sprigs to serve

1/2 cup (70g) slivered almonds

1/4 cup (35g) plain flour

3 cups (750ml) chicken stock

2 sheets puff pastry

1 egg, lightly beaten

1 Preheat oven to 200°C (180°C fan/400°F/Gas 6).

2 Season the chicken with salt and pepper. Heat the olive oil in a 25cm (top measurement), 19cm (base measurement) ovenproof frying pan over a high heat; cook the chicken, in batches, stirring occasionally, for 3 minutes or until browned. Remove the chicken from the pan.

3 Cook the leek in the same pan, stirring occasionally, for 3 minutes or until softened. Add the garlic, thyme, and almonds; cook, stirring, for 1 minute or until fragrant. Return the chicken to the pan with the flour; cook, stirring, for 1 minute. Gradually stir in the stock; bring to the boil. Reduce the heat to low-medium; simmer, stirring occasionally, for 5 minutes or until slightly thickened. Season with salt and pepper to taste. Cool for 10 minutes.

4 Trim the pastry to fit the top of the pan. Cut the pastry off-cuts into decorative shapes. Top the pie with the pastry shapes; brush with egg.

5 Bake the pie for 20 minutes or until the pastry is golden. Serve topped with extra thyme.

TIPS

- The filling can be made, covered, and refrigerated up to 2 days ahead.
- The baked pie can be frozen for up to 3 months.

Spiced lamb pilaf with almonds and currants

PREP + COOK TIME **35 MINUTES + STANDING** | SERVES **4**

Pilaf is a cooked rice dish with its origins in the Middle East. Here the colourful spiced rice is topped with tender fragrant lamb and toasted almonds. Serve with Greek-style yogurt sprinkled with a little ground cumin.

600g lamb tenderloin fillets (see tip)

1 tbsp ground cumin

¼ cup (60ml) olive oil

1 medium red onion (170g), finely chopped

1 medium red capsicum (pepper) (200g), finely chopped

1 stick cinnamon

1 tsp ground allspice

1 bunch fresh coriander

2 cups (400g) basmati rice

4 cups (1 litre) chicken stock

½ cup (80g) currants

2 medium carrots (240g), julienned

½ cup (70g) slivered almonds, toasted

salt and freshly ground black pepper

lemon wedges, to serve

1 Coat the lamb in cumin. Heat a large flameproof frying pan or casserole with a tight-fitting lid over a high heat; add 1 tablespoon of the olive oil. Cook the lamb, turning, for 4 minutes or until browned all over; transfer to a plate. Cover to keep warm.

2 Add the remaining olive oil to the pan, reduce the heat to medium-high; cook the onion and capsicum for 5 minutes or until softened and lightly browned. Add the cinnamon stick and allspice; cook for 30 seconds. Remove the leaves from the coriander bunch; reserve. Finely chop the roots and stems; you will need ⅓ cup. Add to the pan with the rice, stirring to coat the grains well.

3 Add the stock and currants to the pan; bring to the boil. Reduce the heat to low; cook, covered, for 10 minutes. Remove from the heat; stand, covered, for 5 minutes. Discard the cinnamon stick.

4 Slice the lamb thickly on the diagonal; place on top of the rice mixture with the carrot, almonds, and reserved coriander leaves. Season with salt and pepper to taste; serve with lemon wedges.

TIP

Use lamb leg steaks instead of tenderloin fillets, if you prefer.

Chicken quesadillas

PREP + COOK TIME **25 MINUTES** | SERVES **4**

Literally meaning "little cheesy thing", quesadillas originated in Mexico in the 16th century.
They are comprised of two layers of corn or flour tortillas, filled with various ingredients and
grilled to toasty perfection. Serve with sour cream and a baby leaf and cucumber salad.

1 medium avocado (250g), chopped

1 cup (16g) fresh coriander leaves

1 tbsp lemon juice

salt and freshly ground black pepper

1 tbsp vegetable oil

500g minced chicken

2 tsp ground cumin

400g can kidney beans, drained, rinsed

3 medium Roma (plum) tomatoes (225g),
finely chopped

3 green onions (spring onions), thinly sliced

8 x 19cm flour tortillas

1 cup (120g) grated cheddar

lemon wedges, for serving

1   Combine the avocado, coriander, and lemon juice in a small bowl. Season with salt and pepper to taste.

2   Heat the oil in a frying pan; cook the chicken, stirring, until browned. Add the cumin; cook, stirring, for 1 minute or until fragrant. Stir in the kidney beans, tomato, and green onion. Remove the pan from the heat.

3   Preheat sandwich press (see tip).

4   Divide the chicken mixture among four tortillas; sprinkle with the cheddar. Top with the remaining tortillas. Cook one at a time in a sandwich press, for 2 minutes or until the cheddar is melted and the tortillas are lightly browned.

5   Cut the quesadillas into quarters; serve with the avocado mixture and lemon wedges.

TIP

If you don't have a sandwich press, cook these in a
large frying pan or grill pan. Cook one at a time, over
a medium-low heat, for about 2 minutes each side.
Use two spatulas to carefully flip the quesadillas.

Mediterranean fish "pie"

PESCATARIAN | PREP + COOK TIME **1 HOUR 35 MINUTES** | SERVES **4**

Here tender fish is baked in a fragrant tomato-based sauce enlivened with Mediterranean spices and topped with a crunchy sourdough crust. We used blue-eye trevalla, but you can use any of your favourite available white fish fillets instead.

1/4 cup (60ml) olive oil

1 large fennel bulb (550g), cut into 1cm slices, fronds reserved

1 large red onion (300g), cut into thin wedges

2 large garlic cloves, chopped

salt and freshly ground black pepper

1 large red capsicum (pepper) (350g), coarsely chopped

2 celery stalks (300g), coarsely chopped

4 stalks fresh flat-leaf parsley, stalks finely chopped, leaves picked and reserved

3 tsp smoked paprika

1/2 tsp saffron threads

2 tbsp tomato paste

1/2 cup (125ml) dry white wine

4 cups (1 litre) fish stock

400g can cherry tomatoes (see tip)

800g skinless, boneless firm white fish fillets, cut into 3cm pieces

520g day-old garlic sourdough bread, thinly sliced

olive-oil spray

1 tsp finely grated lemon rind

1 Preheat oven to 220°C (200°C fan/425°F/Gas 7).

2 Heat half the olive oil in a 12-cup (3-litre), 30cm round flameproof frying pan or roasting pan over a medium heat. Cook the fennel and onion for 6 minutes, stirring occasionally, until tender. Add the garlic and stir for a further 2 minutes, until lightly browned. Season with salt and pepper; remove the mixture from the pan and set aside.

3 Heat the remaining olive oil in the pan; cook the capsicum, celery, and parsley stalks for 2 minutes or until softened. Add the paprika and saffron; cook for 1 minute. Stir in the tomato paste; cook for a further 1 minute. Increase the heat to high; deglaze the pan with the white wine.

4 Add the stock, tomatoes, and roast vegetable mixture, bring to the boil; boil for 25 minutes or until reduced by a third. Season with salt and pepper to taste.

5 Gently press the fish into the tomato mixture to submerge. Generously spray the sourdough slices with oil; arrange on top of the fish mixture, slightly overlapping in circles. Bake on the top oven shelf for 15 minutes or until the fish is cooked through and the bread is crunchy and golden.

6 Serve the fish pie topped with the reserved fennel fronds, reserved parsley leaves, and lemon rind.

TIP

Swap the canned cherry tomatoes with a 400g can of chopped tomatoes, if preferred.

Vegetable tagine with chickpeas and za'atar

VEGETARIAN | PREP + COOK TIME **1 HOUR** | SERVES **4**

This vibrant tagine is packed with vegetables and Middle Eastern spices. A versatile dish,
it can easily be changed up slightly depending on what vegetables you have in stock.
Serve with rice or crusty bread, if you like.

400g can chickpeas, drained, rinsed

1 tbsp olive oil

1 tbsp za'atar (see tip)

salt and freshly ground black pepper

2 tsp olive oil, extra

1 large red onion (300g), coarsely chopped

2 garlic cloves, crushed

4 baby aubergine (240g), halved lengthways

500g pumpkin, cut into 2cm pieces

2 tsp ground cumin

2 tsp ground coriander

2 tsp ground ginger

1/2 tsp ground cinnamon

400g can cherry tomatoes

2 cups (500ml) vegetable stock

300g baby courgette, trimmed, halved lengthways

3/4 cup (200g) Greek-style yogurt

1/2 cup (10g) finely chopped fresh flat-leaf parsley

1/2 cup (24g) finely chopped fresh mint

1 Pat the chickpeas dry with paper towel. Heat the oil in a large heavy-based saucepan over a medium-high heat; add the chickpeas; cook, stirring frequently for 4 minutes. Stir in the za'atar; season with salt and pepper to taste. Cook for a further 2 minutes or until golden brown and slightly crispy. Remove from the pan and set aside.

2 Heat the extra oil in the same pan over a medium heat; cook the onion and garlic, stirring, for 5 minutes. Add the aubergine and pumpkin; cook for 1 minute on each side or until the vegetables are lightly browned. Add the spices; cook for 1 minute or until fragrant. Add the tomatoes and stock; bring to the boil. Stir in the courgette. Reduce the heat to low; simmer, covered, for 15 minutes or until the vegetables are just tender.

3 Place the yogurt and herbs in a small bowl; stir to combine. Season with salt and pepper to taste.

4 Serve the tagine topped with the yogurt mixture and za'atar chickpeas. Season with pepper. Sprinkle with small mint and flat-leaf parsley leaves, if you like.

TIP

If you don't have the Middle Eastern spice mix za'atar, combine 2 teaspoons dried rigani (Greek oregano) or thyme, 2 teaspoons sesame seeds, and 1/2 teaspoon sumac mixed with a pinch of sea salt.

Crisp-skinned ginger fish

PESCATARIAN | PREP + COOK TIME **30 MINUTES** | SERVES **4**

This healthy and vibrant Thai-inspired dish is packed with flavour and nutrition. Here we've used snapper but you could use any flaky white fish that is available to you. This recipe would also work with chicken instead of fish. Serve with Asian greens such as gai lan.

½ cup (40g) shredded coconut, toasted
vegetable oil, for frying
50g piece fresh ginger, peeled, cut into matchsticks
4 x 200g snapper fillets (or any white fish fillets)
salt
1 green onion (spring onion)
1 tsp finely grated fresh ginger
⅓ cup (80ml) lime juice
⅓ cup (80ml) water
1 tbsp fish sauce
1 small fresh red Thai chilli, thinly sliced
1 tbsp caster sugar

1 Make the coconut rice on page 116.

2 Meanwhile, cook the shredded coconut in a large frying pan, over a medium heat, stirring constantly, until golden. Remove from the pan immediately.

3 Pour enough oil into a large frying pan to cover the bottom. Heat over a medium heat; stir-fry the ginger until golden. Remove with a slotted spoon; drain on paper towel. Combine the ginger and toasted coconut in a small bowl.

4 Carefully pour out the oil leaving 2 tablespoons in the pan. Increase the heat to medium-high. Season the fish on both sides with salt. Cook the fish, skin-side down, for 3 minutes or until golden and crisp; turn the fish over, cook for a further minute or until just cooked through.

5 Slice the green half of the green onion on the diagonal; finely chop the white half.

6 To make the dipping sauce, stir the grated ginger, lime juice, water, fish sauce, chilli, finely chopped green onion, and sugar in a small bowl until the sugar dissolves.

7 Top the fish with the crispy ginger mixture and the remaining green onion. Serve with the coconut rice and ginger dipping sauce.

Side salads

Putting a little thought into your side salads can really elevate a one-pot dish. Here we've given you a selection of vibrant fresh salads to mix and match as appropriate with the dishes you'll find throughout this chapter or beyond.

Classic coleslaw

VEGETARIAN | PREP + COOK TIME **10 MINUTES** | SERVES **4**

Combine 2 tablespoons of mayonnaise, 1 tablespoon of white wine vinegar, and 1 teaspoon of wholegrain mustard. Place a 300g packet of fine cut coleslaw, 1 coarsely grated medium carrot, and 3 thinly sliced green onions (spring onions) in a large bowl with the dressing; toss gently to combine.

Simple green salad

VEGETARIAN | PREP + COOK TIME **5 MINUTES** | SERVES **4**

Place 100g mixed salad leaves in a bowl. Top with 1 large coarsely chopped avocado and 4 thickly sliced baby cucumbers. Combine 1 tablespoon of extra-virgin olive oil with 2 teaspoons of red wine vinegar, and 1 teaspoon of Dijon mustard in a small bowl. Season with salt and pepper to taste. Drizzle over the salad.

Lemony lettuce wedges

VEGETARIAN | PREP + COOK TIME **5 MINUTES** | SERVES **4**

Combine 1/2 cup (150g) each of sour cream and mayonnaise, 1/2 teaspoon of finely grated lemon rind, and 3 teaspoons of lemon juice in a small bowl. Season with salt and pepper to taste. Wash and drain 2 quartered baby cos lettuces. Place on a platter. Spoon the mayonnaise mixture over the lettuce. Scatter with 1 tablespoon of chopped fresh chives and extra lemon zest.

Perfect potato salad

VEGETARIAN | PREP + COOK TIME **20 MINUTES** | SERVES **6**

Cut 1.5kg potatoes into large pieces. Boil, microwave, or steam the potato until tender; drain. Transfer to a large bowl; drizzle over 2 tablespoons of apple cider vinegar. Toss gently to combine. Add 1/2 cup (150g) mayonnaise combined with 2 teaspoons of horseradish cream. Stir in 2 tablespoons each of coarsely chopped fresh mint and dill. Season with salt and pepper to taste. Scatter with extra mint; serve.

Lemon fish with fennel and capers

PESCATARIAN | PREP + COOK TIME **25 MINUTES** | SERVES **4**

This fragrant zesty fish dish is healthy, delicious, and ready in under half an hour. We used
blue-eye trevalla for this recipe but you can use any firm white fish fillets you like – swordfish
would be a good substitute. Serve with a green salad.

4 baby fennel bulbs (520g)

2 tbsp olive oil

1 medium lemon (140g), thinly sliced

4 x 180g skinless firm white fish fillets

salt and freshly ground black pepper

275g baby Roma (plum) tomatoes, halved lengthways

2 tbsp drained, rinsed capers

1/4 cup (60ml) dry white wine

30g butter, chopped

1 Trim the fennel, reserve the fronds; cut the fennel into wedges. Heat
the olive oil in a large frying pan; cook the fennel until lightly browned
on both sides.

2 Add the lemon to the pan; cook until lightly browned and tender.

3 Season the fish with salt and pepper, add to the pan, pushing the
fennel and lemon to the side of the pan; cook the fish until browned
on both sides.

4 Add the tomato, capers, and wine to the pan; bring to the boil. Dot the
fish with butter; sprinkle with half the reserved fennel fronds. Reduce
the heat; cook, covered, for 5 minutes or until the fish is just cooked
through. Season with salt and pepper to taste.

5 Serve the fish drizzled with the pan juices and sprinkled with the
remaining fennel fronds.

"Courgetti" and meatballs

PREP + COOK TIME **40 MINUTES** | SERVES **4**

Spaghetti-like strands are created from courgette in this recipe, and used instead of actual pasta, making it a great gluten-free option. If you prefer, cook the sausages whole then slice and add to the tomato mixture.

750g gluten-free beef sausages

2 garlic cloves, crushed

450g mixed baby heirloom tomatoes, halved if large

2 cups (560g) bottled tomato passata

1/4 cup (5g) coarsely chopped fresh basil

salt and freshly ground black pepper

6 medium courgette (900g) (see tip)

1/2 cup (40g) finely grated parmesan

1 Squeeze the meat from the sausages. Add the garlic; mix to combine. Roll the mixture into balls.

2 Cook the meatballs in an oiled large frying pan, over a medium-high heat, for 3 minutes or until browned all over. Add the tomatoes, passata, and half the basil; bring to the boil. Reduce the heat; simmer for 5 minutes or until the meatballs are cooked through. Season with salt and pepper.

3 Meanwhile, using a julienne peeler or spiralizer (see tip), cut the courgette into "spaghetti".

4 Add the courgette and half the parmesan to the sauce mixture; stir gently. Serve the "courgetti" and meatballs sprinkled with the remaining basil and parmesan.

TIP

If you don't have a julienne peeler or a spiralizer, simply use a vegetable peeler to thinly slice the courgette lengthways into ribbons, then stack and slice into long thin strips using a large straight-bladed knife.

Rainbow chard and three-cheese frittata

VEGETARIAN | PREP + COOK TIME **15 MINUTES** | SERVES **4**

We cooked the frittata mixture in two smaller frying pans, but you can make one bigger
frittata in a large 25cm (base measurement) frying pan; cook the frittata, over a medium-low
heat, for 10 minutes at step 4, then cook under the grill as the recipe suggests.

40g butter

375g rainbow chard, trimmed,
coarsely shredded

8 eggs

²/₃ cup (50g) finely grated pecorino cheese

salt and freshly ground black pepper

50g Gorgonzola cheese, crumbled

50g firm ricotta

100g rocket leaves

1 tbsp olive oil

1 tbsp lemon juice

¹/₄ cup (20g) grated pecorino cheese, extra

1   Preheat the grill.

2   Melt half the butter between two 20cm (base measurement) frying pans
    over a high heat. Divide the rainbow chard between pans; cook, stirring,
    until wilted. Remove from the pans; drain well.

3   Combine the eggs, rainbow chard, and pecorino in a large jug; season
    with sea salt and freshly ground black pepper.

4   Melt the remaining butter in the same pans; pour, or spoon, equal
    amounts of the egg mixture into the pans, top evenly with the Gorgonzola
    and ricotta. Cook, over a medium-low heat, for 5 minutes or until the
    frittatas are almost set. Place the frittatas under the grill; grill for
    5 minutes or until set and lightly browned.

5   Combine the rocket, olive oil, lemon juice, and extra pecorino in a
    medium bowl; serve with the frittatas.

TIP

You need ovenproof frying pans for this recipe;
or wrap the handles of your frying pans with a
few layers of foil to protect them from the heat
of the grill.

Tofu larb with crisp rice papers

VEGETARIAN | PREP + COOK TIME **30 MINUTES** | SERVES **4**

Larb is a refreshing and spicy Thai salad traditionally made with minced pork or chicken and served in crisp green leaves. Our fragrant vegan version instead uses tofu and coarsely chopped walnuts for added bite.

250g firm tofu

4 green onions (spring onions)

⅓ cup (80ml) lime juice

¼ cup (60ml) vegetable stock

2 tbsp soy sauce

1½ tbsp brown sugar

2 tbsp vegetable oil

1 fresh long red chilli, seeded, finely chopped

1 stalk lemongrass, white part only, thinly sliced

1 tbsp finely chopped fresh ginger

1 cup (100g) coarsely chopped roasted walnuts

2 tbsp finely chopped fresh coriander

1 gem lettuce (180g), leaves separated

1 fresh long red chilli, thinly sliced, extra

lime wedges, to serve (optional)

crisp rice papers

½ cup (125ml) vegetable oil

8 x 16cm rice paper rounds

1 To make the crisp rice papers, heat the oil in a large frying pan over a medium-high heat. Cook one rice paper at a time for 30 seconds or until puffed. Drain on paper towel. Drain any excess oil from the pan.

2 Pat the tofu dry with paper towel. Crumble the tofu into small chunks. Thinly slice the white part of the green onions. Shred the green tops; reserve to serve.

3 Place the lime juice, stock, soy sauce, and sugar in a small jug; stir until the sugar dissolves. Pour half the sauce mixture into a small dipping bowl; reserve to serve.

4 Heat the oil in the same large frying pan over a high heat; stir-fry the tofu for 8 minutes or until golden. Add the white part of the green onion, chopped chilli, lemongrass, and ginger; stir-fry for 1 minute or until fragrant. Add the walnuts; stir-fry for 30 seconds. Add the remaining sauce mixture to the pan; bring to a simmer, cook for 2 minutes or until reduced by half. Stir in the coriander. Keep warm.

5 Serve the larb on the lettuce leaves, with the reserved sauce and crisp rice papers, topped with the reserved green onion and extra sliced chilli. Serve with lime wedges, if using.

Prawn saganaki

PESCATARIAN | PREP + COOK TIME **40 MINUTES** | SERVES **4**

Saganaki is a popular Greek dish, named after a *sagani*, the two-handled frying pan in which it is cooked and served. Traditionally made with grilled or fried cheese, sprinkled with lemon juice, and eaten with bread, saganaki has evolved to include meat, and/or seafood.

1kg uncooked medium king prawns

1 medium lemon (140g)

2 tbsp olive oil

400g spring onions, trimmed, quartered

2 garlic cloves, finely chopped

1/2 cup (125ml) dry white wine

1/2 tsp caster sugar

400g can whole tomatoes

few drops Tabasco

1/2 cup (10g) coarsely chopped fresh flat-leaf parsley

1/3 cup (3g) fresh dill sprigs

1/3 cup (3g) fresh mint leaves

180g feta cheese

salt and freshly ground black pepper

1   Shell and devein the prawns, leaving tails intact.

2   Finely grate the lemon rind; segment the lemon.

3   Heat the olive oil in a large frying pan; cook the onion and garlic, stirring, until softened. Add the prawns; cook, stirring, until the prawns begin to change colour. Add the wine, sugar, tomatoes, Tabasco, and half the herbs; bring to the boil. Reduce the heat to a simmer.

4   Place the lemon segments and crumbled feta on top of the prawns, sprinkle with the lemon rind; cook, covered, for 3 minutes or until the cheese begins to melt. Season with salt and pepper to taste. Serve sprinkled with the remaining herbs.

WOK

From spicy stir-fries to fragrant curries,
these Asian-inspired vibrant dishes show
that one-pot cooking doesn't have to be
one-dimensional.

Pineapple pork stir-fry

PREP + COOK TIME **25 MINUTES** | SERVES **2**

This sweet and spicy stir-fry will take your weeknight suppers to a new level. Sriracha is a Thai-style chilli sauce available from most supermarkets and Asian food stores. Substitute with whatever chilli sauce you have on hand, or use a little fresh seeded chilli instead.

250g can pineapple pieces in natural juice

200g pork fillet, thinly sliced

2 tsp finely grated fresh ginger

1 tbsp light soy sauce

2 tsp Sriracha

1 garlic clove, crushed

2 tbsp vegetable oil

220g shelf fresh udon noodles

210g broccolini (Tenderstem broccoli), sliced

1 small onion (80g), thinly sliced

1 fresh long red chilli, thinly sliced

125g baby corn, halved lengthways

¼ cup (60ml) water

2 tbsp chopped salted roasted peanuts

1 Drain the pineapple juice into a medium bowl; reserve the pineapple. Add the pork, ginger, soy sauce, Sriracha, garlic, and 1 tablespoon of the oil to the bowl; stir to combine. Stand for 10 minutes.

2 Place the noodles in a heatproof bowl, cover with boiling water. Stir the noodles to separate, stand for 1 minute; drain.

3 Drain the pork from the marinade, reserving the marinade. Heat 2 teaspoons of the oil in a wok over a medium-high heat; stir-fry the pork for 2 minutes or until browned. Remove from the pan.

4 Heat the remaining oil in the wok, add the broccolini, onion, chilli, and corn; stir-fry for 2 minutes. Add the reserved marinade and the water, bring to the boil; boil for 3 minutes or until the vegetables are tender. Add the pineapple, noodles, and pork; stir-fry for 2 minutes. Divide into bowls; sprinkle with peanuts to serve.

Seafood chu chee curry

PESCATARIAN | PREP + COOK TIME **15 MINUTES** | SERVES **4**

Chu chee is a Thai red curry that can be made with any kind of seafood. Chu chee curry is from the Southern and Central areas of Thailand and the name is derived from the sound of the spice paste frying in the pan.

1/4 cup (60g) ghee

2 1/2 tbsp Thai red curry paste

800g marinara (seafood) mix

6 fresh makrut lime leaves

270ml canned coconut milk

1 cup (250ml) fish stock

2 tbsp coconut sugar (or palm sugar)

2 tbsp fish sauce

1 tbsp tamarind puree

225g can bamboo shoots, drained, rinsed

1/2 cup (85g) chopped fresh pineapple

1 fresh long red chilli, seeded, finely sliced

4 roti bread (500g), warmed

steamed jasmine rice, to serve

1 Heat a wok over a medium-high heat. Add the ghee and curry paste; cook, stirring, for 2 minutes or until fragrant. Add the marinara mix and 3 crushed lime leaves; cook, stirring, for 2 minutes.

2 Add the coconut milk, stock, sugar, fish sauce, and tamarind. Stir in the bamboo shoots and pineapple; cook for a further 5 minutes or until the mixture is heated through.

3 Finely shred the remaining lime leaves; combine with the chilli. Sprinkle the lime leaf mixture over the curry; serve with steamed jasmine rice and warm roti bread.

Veggie pad thai

VEGETARIAN | PREP + COOK TIME **40 MINUTES + STANDING** | SERVES **6**

Bring a taste of Thailand and a splash of colour to your table with a vibrant veggie pad thai.
Healthy and bursting with flavour, this easy-to-cook noodle stir-fry has a delicious
sweet, savoury, and nutty sauce that's a treat for your tastebuds.

200g dried rice noodles

$^1/_3$ cup (80ml) peanut oil

$^1/_4$ cup (60ml) boiling water

$^1/_2$ cup (135g) grated palm sugar or brown sugar

1 tbsp tamarind puree

$^1/_4$ cup (60ml) lime juice

$^1/_3$ cup (80ml) gluten-free tamari

400g packaged fresh stir-fry vegetable mix

3 eggs, lightly beaten

2 garlic cloves, crushed

4 green onions (spring onions), thinly sliced diagonally

$^2/_3$ cup (100g) roasted unsalted peanuts,
coarsely chopped

$^1/_3$ cup (25g) fried Asian shallots

150g bean sprouts

$^1/_2$ cup (8g) coriander leaves

lime halves, to serve

1   Place the noodles in a large heatproof bowl; cover with boiling water.
Stand for 15 minutes or until just tender. Drain the noodles, toss with
2 teaspoons of the oil; cover with plastic wrap (cling film) to prevent
them drying out.

2   Stir the boiling water, sugar, tamarind, lime juice, and tamari in a small
jug until the sugar dissolves.

3   Heat a wok over a high heat; add 1 tablespoon of the peanut oil. Add the
vegetable mix; stir-fry for about 2 minutes or until the vegetables are
tender. Remove from the wok.

4   Add the egg to the wok; swirl to coat the bottom and side. Cook the egg
until just set; transfer to a board, then chop coarsely.

5   Heat the remaining oil and garlic in the wok; stir-fry until the garlic
is fragrant. Return the vegetables to the wok with the noodles,
three-quarters of the green onion, and the sauce mixture; stir-fry until
the noodles are heated through. Stir in the chopped egg.

6   Remove from the heat. Sprinkle over half the peanuts and half the
shallots; toss to combine.

7   Serve the noodles topped with the bean sprouts, coriander, the remaining
peanuts, green onion, and shallots; serve the pad thai with lime halves.

Hoisin beef and shiitake stir-fry

PREP + COOK TIME **35 MINUTES + REFRIGERATION** | SERVES **4**

Tender strips of marinated beef and sir-fried mushrooms create a wonderfully full-bodied sweet and sour dish, easy to whip up for a midweek dinner. Serve with either steamed rice or tricolour quinoa.

1 tsp sesame oil

2 garlic cloves, crushed

1 tsp finely grated fresh ginger

1/3 cup (80ml) Chinese cooking wine (shao hsing)

1/3 cup (80ml) soy sauce

800g beef rump steak, thinly sliced against the grain

1 tbsp vegetable oil

100g fresh shiitake mushrooms, trimmed

500g choy sum, leaves and stems separated, cut into 5cm lengths

4 green onions (spring onions), cut into 5cm lengths

1/4 cup (60ml) water

1/4 cup (60ml) hoisin sauce

100g tong ho (edible chrysanthemum) (optional, see tips)

snow pea sprouts (pea shoots), to serve (optional)

1 fresh long red chilli, seeded, julienned

1 Combine the sesame oil, garlic, ginger, half the rice wine, and half the soy sauce in a large bowl. Add the beef; toss to coat in the marinade. Cover; refrigerate for 3 hours or overnight.

2 Heat a wok over a high heat, add half the vegetable oil; stir-fry the undrained beef mixture, in batches, until the beef is browned and just cooked through. Transfer to a bowl.

3 Heat the remaining vegetable oil in the wok; stir-fry the mushrooms, choy sum stalks, and green onion. Add the water. Cover; cook for 5 minutes or until the vegetables are tender.

4 Return the beef to the wok with the hoisin sauce, choy sum leaves, tong ho, if using, remaining rice wine, and remaining soy sauce; stir-fry until the leaves just wilt.

5 Serve the stir-fry topped with the snow pea sprouts, if using, and chilli.

TIPS

- Tong ho is an edible form of chrysanthemum available from Asian food stores; if unavailable use gai lan or spinach leaves instead.
- Beef can be marinated a day ahead; cover and refrigerate.

Sichuan mapo tofu

PREP + COOK TIME **25 MINUTES** | SERVES **4**

This popular Chinese dish from the Sichuan region of China is rich, aromatic, and brimming with fiery flavour. It should have plenty of *mala*, a numbing kind of spiciness that is a characteristic of great Sichuan cuisine.

2 tsp Sichuan peppercorns

1 tbsp cornflour

1/4 cup (60ml) Chinese cooking wine (shao hsing)

1 cup (250ml) chicken stock

2 tsp light soy sauce

3 tsp white (granulated) sugar

1/2 cup (125ml) water

1 tbsp sesame oil

4 garlic cloves, crushed

300g minced pork

2 tbsp chilli bean paste (see tips)

300g fresh silken tofu, drained, cut into 2cm cubes

1/4 cup (35g) roasted peanuts, coarsely chopped

2 green onions (spring onions), thinly sliced

1 Stir the peppercorns in a wok over a medium heat for 1 minute or until fragrant. Crush lightly using a pestle and mortar. (Alternatively, place on a chopping board and crush with the base of a clean, heavy-based saucepan.)

2 Whisk the cornflour, cooking wine, stock, soy sauce, sugar, and water in a medium jug until combined.

3 Heat the sesame oil in a wok over a high heat. Add the garlic and pork; stir-fry for 8 minutes or until the pork is browned. Stir in the chilli bean paste and half the peppercorns; stir-fry the mixture for a further minute.

4 Stir the cornflour mixture into the pork mixture in the wok; cook until the mixture boils and thickens slightly. Reduce the heat to medium; cook for 5 minutes. Carefully add the tofu and stir gently to combine. Cook for a further 2 minutes or until heated through.

5 Divide the ma po tofu among 4 bowls; top with the peanuts, green onion, and remaining crushed peppercorns. Serve with steamed white rice, if you like.

TIPS

• Chilli bean paste and Sichuan peppercorns are available from Asian food stores.
• To make a vegetarian version of the recipe, omit the pork and double the tofu.

Fragrant beef curry with crisp coconut topping

PREP + COOK TIME **50 MINUTES** | SERVES **4**

The crisp coconut topping, originating in Indonesia and also known as serundeng, is usually sprinkled over a hot dish just as it's served, much like a gremolata, to awaken the tastebuds. Alternatively, it can be served as a condiment to accompany rice.

2 tbsp vegetable oil

750g beef strips

1 medium onion (150g), finely chopped

3 garlic cloves, crushed

10cm stalk fresh lemongrass (20g), finely chopped

1 star anise

1 cinnamon stick

270ml can coconut cream

1 tbsp tamarind puree

200g green beans, trimmed, halved lengthways

1 tbsp fish sauce

$1/2$ cup (8g) fresh coriander leaves

450g cooked jasmine rice

crisp coconut topping

2 tbsp vegetable oil

4 green onions (spring onions), chopped

2 cups (100g) flaked coconut

2 tbsp brown sugar

$1/4$ cup (75g) tamarind puree

1 Make the crisp coconut topping. Heat the oil in a wok over a medium-high heat; add the remaining ingredients; stir-fry, tossing continuously, for 15–20 minutes or until crisp and browned. Remove from the wok.

2 Heat half the oil in the wok over a high heat; stir-fry the beef, in batches, until browned. Remove from the wok; cover to keep warm.

3 Heat the remaining oil in the wok; stir-fry the onion until soft. Add the garlic, lemongrass, star anise, and cinnamon; stir-fry until fragrant. Add the coconut cream and tamarind; cook, stirring occasionally, for 5 minutes or until the mixture has thickened slightly. Return the beef to the wok with the green beans and fish sauce; stir-fry for 3 minutes or until the beans are just tender. Remove from the heat; stir in the coriander. Remove and discard the cinnamon stick before serving.

4 Stir three-quarters of the crisp coconut topping through the warmed jasmine rice; sprinkle the remaining topping over the curry. Serve the curry with the rice.

Rice

Rice is the perfect accompaniment to Asian-inspired dishes cooked in a wok. Whilst plain steamed rice has an important role, it can be fun to experiment with rice sides, bringing in your favourite flavours to keep things interesting.

Coconut rice

VEGAN | PREP + COOK TIME **20 MINUTES** | SERVES **4**

Place 1½ cups (300g) jasmine rice, 270ml canned coconut milk, ⅔ cup (170ml) water, and 2 teaspoons of finely grated fresh ginger in a heavy-based saucepan, season with salt; stir well to combine. Cover the pan with a lid; bring to the boil over a medium heat. Reduce the heat to low; cook for 10 minutes. Turn off the heat; stand, covered, for a further 5 minutes before removing the lid.

Basmati pilaf

PREP + COOK TIME **30 MINUTES** | SERVES **4**

Melt 20g butter in a medium saucepan; cook 1 crushed garlic clove, stirring, until fragrant. Add 1 cup (200g) brown basmati rice; cook, stirring, for 1 minute. Add 1 cup (250ml) chicken stock and 1 cup (250ml) water; bring to the boil. Reduce the heat to low; simmer, covered, for 20 minutes or until the rice is just tender. Remove from the heat; fluff the rice with a fork. Stir in ¼ cup (5g) coarsely chopped fresh flat-leaf parsley and ¼ cup (35g) toasted flaked almonds.

Cauliflower "rice" pilaf

VEGAN | PREP + COOK TIME **20 MINUTES** | SERVES **4**

Process 1 coarsely chopped medium (1kg) cauliflower, in batches, until finely chopped. Heat 2 tablespoons of olive oil in a large heavy-based frying pan over a high heat. Add 1 teaspoon of cumin seeds and the cauliflower to a frying pan; cook, stirring occasionally, for 12 minutes or until the cauliflower is just tender. Stir in ¼ cup (8g) coarsely chopped fresh coriander; season with salt and pepper to taste.

Steamed ginger rice

PREP + COOK TIME **20 MINUTES** | SERVES **4**

Heat 1 tablespoon of olive oil in a medium heavy-based saucepan; cook 6 thinly sliced green onions (spring onions), stirring, until softened. Add 2½ teaspoons of finely grated fresh ginger and 1½ cups (300g) basmati rice; stir to coat in oil. Add 2 cups (500ml) chicken stock; bring to the boil. Reduce the heat; simmer, covered, over a low heat for 10 minutes. Remove from the heat; stand, covered, for 5 minutes, then fluff with a fork. Stir in 2 tablespoons of finely chopped fresh mint; season with salt and pepper to taste.

Stir-fried chicken with tamari almond crumble

PREP + COOK TIME **35 MINUTES + STANDING AND COOLING** | SERVES **4**

You can marinate the chicken in a covered bowl in the fridge for 2 hours or overnight, if you like. This will help keep the chicken moist and bring in a greater depth of flavour. Serve with steamed rice and extra sliced green onion (spring onion).

2 tbsp light soy sauce

1 tbsp Chinese cooking wine (shao hsing)

1 tbsp sea salt flakes

1 tsp white (granulated) sugar

600g chicken breast fillets, thickly sliced on the diagonal

1/4 cup (60ml) vegetable oil

4 trimmed celery stalks (400g), cut into 4cm lengths on the diagonal

2 fresh long red chillies, thinly sliced

200g snow peas (mangetout), halved lengthways

5cm piece fresh ginger, peeled, julienned

2 garlic cloves, thinly sliced

4 green onions (spring onions), thinly sliced

1/4 tsp sesame oil

tamari almond crumble

1/4 cup (40g) tamari almonds

1 1/2 tbsp white sesame seeds

1/4 cup (8g) finely chopped fresh coriander

1 Combine 1 tablespoon of the soy sauce, the cooking wine, salt, and sugar in a medium bowl; add the chicken. Toss the chicken to coat in the marinade. Cover; stand for 15 minutes for the flavours to develop.

2 Meanwhile, make the tamari almond crumble. Place the almonds and sesame seeds in a dry wok over a medium heat. Cook, shaking the wok, for 2 minutes or until the sesame seeds are golden. Transfer to a bowl; cool. Process the almond mixture until chopped coarsely. Add the coriander and pulse until just combined. Transfer to a small bowl.

3 Heat 1 tablespoon of the vegetable oil in the wok over high heat. Add the celery and chilli; stir-fry for 3 minutes or until just tender. Stir through 1 tablespoon of the soy sauce; transfer to a large plate.

4 Rinse the wok; wipe clean. Heat another 1 tablespoon of the oil in the wok over a high heat; add the chicken, discard the marinade. Stir-fry the chicken for 8 minutes or until browned and cooked through. Transfer to a bowl.

5 Add the remaining oil to the wok, add the snow peas, ginger, garlic, and green onion; stir-fry for 2 minutes or until aromatic. Return the chicken to the wok with the sesame oil; stir to combine.

6 Combine the chicken mixture and vegetables, sprinkle with the tamari almond crumble.

Stir-fried prawn omelette

PREP + COOK TIME **15 MINUTES** | SERVES **2**

Pieces of omelette are broken up and stir-fried with prawns and bean sprouts in this fresh and flavourful recipe. So quick and easy to prepare, yet delivering on taste and nutrition, it's sure to become a weeknight staple.

300g uncooked medium king prawns (see tip)

1 tbsp peanut oil

4 eggs, lightly beaten

4 green onions (spring onions), cut into 6cm lengths

1 garlic clove, finely chopped

2cm piece fresh ginger (10g), grated

¼ cup (60ml) chicken stock

1 tsp soy sauce

salt and freshly ground pepper

1 cup (80g) bean sprouts

1 Shell and devein the prawns, leaving the tails intact.

2 Heat half the oil in a wok. Pour the egg into the wok; cook the omelette, tilting the wok, until almost set. Remove the omelette from the wok; cover to keep warm.

3 Heat the remaining oil in the wok; stir-fry the prawns, green onion, garlic, and ginger until the prawns change colour.

4 Add the stock and soy sauce to the wok; bring to the boil. Return the omelette to the wok; stir-fry until hot, breaking the omelette into pieces. Season with salt and pepper. Remove from the heat; stir in the bean sprouts.

TIP

To save time, you could purchase 150g shelled prawns for this recipe.

Salt and pepper calamari

PESCATARIAN | PREP + COOK TIME **25 MINUTES** | SERVES **4**

Perfect for an al fresco lunch on a summer's day, this calamari is cooked quickly to ensure it's
light and crispy on the outside, and melt-in-the-mouth succulent on the inside. For a
gluten-free option, use gluten-free plain flour.

$^1/_3$ cup (50g) plain flour

$1^1/_2$ tsp sea salt flakes

$1^1/_2$ tsp cracked black pepper

vegetable oil, for deep-frying

2kg baby calamari, cleaned, hoods sliced into rings

80g baby rocket leaves

1 small red onion (100g), thinly sliced

250g baby cucumbers, thinly sliced lengthways
(see tip)

lemon halves, to serve

lemon aïoli

$1^1/_2$ cups (450g) whole-egg mayonnaise

2 tsp finely grated lemon rind

2 tbsp lemon juice

1 garlic clove, crushed

1 Make the lemon aïoli. Combine the ingredients in a small bowl.

2 Combine the flour, salt, and pepper in a large bowl.

3 Fill a large wok one-third full with oil; heat to 180°C/350°F (or until a
cube of bread turns golden in 15 seconds). Working in batches, toss the
calamari in the flour mixture; shake away excess. Fry the calamari for
2 minutes or until golden and just tender; drain on paper towel.

4 Combine the rocket, onion, and cucumber in a large bowl. Serve the
calamari with the rocket salad, aïoli, and lemon halves.

TIP

Use a vegetable peeler to slice the cucumbers
lengthways into long thin ribbons.

Chicken fried rice

PREP + COOK TIME **25 MINUTES** | SERVES **4**

This is a versatile recipe and you can easily replace the capsicum (pepper), cabbage, and mushrooms with other vegetables you have on hand; simply ensure that they are cut into thin slices. You can serve the rice sprinkled with Asian fried shallots for added texture, if you like.

2 tbsp vegetable oil

2 eggs, lightly beaten

4 chicken thigh fillets (800g), thinly sliced

1/2 medium red capsicum (pepper) (100g), thinly sliced

1 small red onion (100g), thinly sliced

2 cups (160g) chopped cabbage

150g oyster mushrooms, coarsely chopped

3 garlic cloves, crushed

1/2 tsp dried chilli flakes

2 x 250g packets microwave white basmati rice

1 tsp sesame oil

2 tbsp soy sauce

2 green onions (spring onions), thinly sliced

1/4 cup (60ml) sweet chilli sauce

2 tbsp fresh coriander leaves

1 Heat 1 teaspoon of the vegetable oil in a large wok over a high heat. Pour the egg into the wok; cook, tilting the wok, until the omelette is just set. Remove the omelette from the wok; chop coarsely.

2 Heat 3 teaspoons of the remaining oil in the wok; stir-fry the chicken for 2 minutes or until browned. Remove from the wok.

3 Heat the remaining oil in the wok; stir-fry the capsicum, red onion, cabbage, mushrooms, garlic, and chilli for 3 minutes or until the vegetables soften.

4 Return the chicken and egg to the wok with the rice, sesame oil, soy sauce, half the green onion, and 2 tablespoons of the sweet chilli sauce; stir-fry until heated through. (Taste the fried rice and add extra soy sauce if required.)

5 Serve the rice drizzled with the remaining sweet chilli sauce and sprinkled with coriander and the remaining green onion.

TIP

If you'd prefer to cook your own rice, do it several hours ahead or the day before. You will need to cook 1 cup (200g) of rice, following the packet directions, to yield 3 cups (500g) of cooked rice.

Gado-gado tempeh stir-fry lettuce cups

VEGETARIAN | PREP + COOK TIME **30 MINUTES** | SERVES **4**

Use a sugar-free peanut butter for the sauce and serve sprinkled with coarsely chopped roasted peanuts and extra sliced green onion (spring onion), if you like. You could also use iceberg or baby cos lettuce leaves instead of butter (round) lettuce, if you prefer.

$\frac{1}{2}$ cup (140g) smooth peanut butter

$\frac{1}{2}$ cup (125ml) coconut milk

$\frac{1}{4}$ cup (60ml) water

2 tbsp light soy sauce

1 garlic clove, crushed

1 fresh long red chilli, seeded, finely chopped

$\frac{1}{2}$ cup (125ml) vegetable oil

250g tempeh, diced

300g broccoli, cut into small florets, stalks finely chopped

1 medium carrot (120g), thinly sliced

300g snow peas (mangetout), trimmed

3 green onions (spring onions), thinly sliced

4 eggs

8 butter (round) lettuce leaves

freshly ground black pepper

lemon wedges, to serve

1 Whisk the peanut butter, coconut milk, water, soy sauce, garlic, and half the chilli until combined.

2 Heat 2 tablespoons of the oil in a large wok over a high heat. Stir-fry the tempeh for 5 minutes or until golden. Transfer to a large bowl; keep warm.

3 Heat another 2 tablespoons of oil in the wok. Stir-fry the broccoli, carrot, snow peas, and green onion for 4 minutes or until tender. Add $\frac{1}{4}$ cup (60ml) of the sauce and toss to coat the vegetables. Transfer the vegetable mixture to the bowl of tempeh; stir gently to mix.

4 Heat the remaining oil, 2 tablespoons of the sauce, and the remaining chilli in a wok over a medium heat. Fry the eggs for 3 minutes or until the whites are firm, edges are crisp, and the yolks are cooked to your liking.

5 Divide the lettuce cups, tempeh mixture, and chilli-fried eggs among 4 plates; drizzle with the remaining sauce. Season with pepper; serve with lemon wedges.

Chow mein

PREP + COOK TIME **25 MINUTES** | SERVES **4**

Chow mein, meaning "stir-fried noodles", hails from Northern China. While the dish has been altered over the years and across the globe to appeal to different tastes, its base is stir-fried vegetables and noodles. Here chicken or pork could be used instead of turkey.

1 tbsp peanut oil

500g minced turkey

1 medium red onion (170g), finely chopped

2 garlic cloves, crushed

1 tbsp mild curry powder

2 stalks celery (300g), trimmed, finely chopped

1 medium carrot (120g), coarsely grated

1/4 cup (60ml) reduced-salt chicken stock

2 tbsp oyster sauce

1 tbsp soy sauce

2 cups (160g) finely shredded wombok (Chinese leaf)

1 cup (120g) frozen baby peas

100g fried noodles

1/3 cup (55g) coarsely chopped roasted blanched almonds

2 green onions (spring onions), thinly sliced

1 Heat the oil in a wok; stir-fry the turkey, red onion, and garlic until the turkey changes colour. Add the curry powder; stir-fry until fragrant. Add the celery and carrot; stir-fry until the vegetables are tender. Add the stock, oyster sauce, soy sauce, wombok, and peas; stir-fry until the wombok wilts.

2 Serve the stir-fry sprinkled with the noodles, almonds, and green onion.

Five spice salt and pepper prawn stir-fry

PESCATARIAN | PREP + COOK TIME **35 MINUTES** | SERVES **4**

Chinese five spice powder is an aromatic blend of five spices. Although there are many variations to the spices used, the most conventional ones are cloves, fennel seeds, Chinese cinnamon, Sichuan peppercorns, and star anise.

2 tsp sea salt flakes

2 tsp freshly ground black pepper

1 tsp Chinese five spice powder

1 cup (120g) cornflour

1 cup (250ml) vegetable oil

1kg uncooked prawns, peeled, deveined, tails intact

¼ cup (60ml) lime juice

1 tbsp fish sauce

1 tbsp brown sugar

1 tbsp vegetable oil, extra

2 garlic cloves, finely chopped

1 fresh long red chilli, thinly sliced

1 stem fresh lemongrass, white part only, finely chopped

3 green onions (spring onions), sliced

1 bunch broccolini (Tenderstem broccoli) (175g), trimmed, halved lengthways

1 medium carrot (120g), julienned

100g daikon, peeled, julienned

100g snow peas (mangetout)

sliced fresh red chilli and micro radish leaves, to serve (optional)

1   Combine the salt flakes, pepper, and five spice in a small bowl. Place the cornflour in another bowl, add half the spice mixture; stir to combine.

2   Heat the vegetable oil in a wok or large heavy-based frying pan over a medium-high heat. Toss the prawns in the cornflour mixture to coat; shake away the excess. Working in batches, stir-fry the prawns for 3 minutes or until crisp and cooked through. Transfer to a paper towel-lined tray to absorb the excess oil.

3   For the dressing, place the lime juice, fish sauce, and sugar in a screw-top jar; shake well.

4   Drain the wok; wipe clean. Add the extra oil and heat over a medium-high heat. Add the garlic, chilli, lemongrass, and green onion; stir-fry for 2 minutes. Add the broccolini, carrot, and daikon; stir-fry for 2 minutes. Add the snow peas; stir-fry for a further 1 minute. Add the prawns and half the dressing; stir-fry for 1 minute or until warmed through.

5   Sprinkle the prawn stir-fry with the remaining spiced salt; top with the chilli and micro leaves, if using. Serve with the remaining dressing.

Easy veggie sides

Putting a little thought into your vegetable sides can really elevate a one-pot dish. Here we've given you a selection of sides to mix and match as appropriate with the dishes you'll find throughout this chapter and beyond.

Shake and bake wedges

VEGAN | PREP + COOK TIME **50 MINUTES** | SERVES **4**

Preheat oven to 220°C (200°C fan/425°F/Gas 7). Line a large oven tray with baking paper; brush the paper with 1 tablespoon of olive oil. Cut 2 small sweet potatoes, 2 large parsnips, and 2 large potatoes into wedges; toss with 1 teaspoon each of smoked paprika and sea salt flakes. Spread the wedges over the tray. Bake for 40 minutes or until tender.

Steamed Asian greens

PESCATARIAN | PREP + COOK TIME **15 MINUTES** | SERVES **4**

Layer 350g trimmed broccolini (Tenderstem broccoli), 2 halved baby bok choy (pak choi), and 1 thinly sliced fresh long red chilli in a large baking-paper-lined bamboo steamer. Steam, covered, over a wok of simmering water for 5 minutes or until the vegetables are just tender. Combine 2 tablespoons of oyster sauce and 2 tablespoons of boiling water in a bowl; drizzle over the vegetables. Scatter with 1 teaspoon of toasted sesame seeds.

Minted greens

VEGAN | PREP + COOK TIME **10 MINUTES** | SERVES **4**

Cook 200g trimmed green beans and 200g sugar snap peas in a saucepan of boiling water for 3 minutes; drain, then transfer to a bowl. Combine ½ cup (24g) finely chopped fresh mint and 2 tablespoons of extra virgin olive oil in a small bowl. Toss the vegetables with the mint mixture; season with salt and pepper to taste. Serve scattered with a few extra mint leaves, if you like.

Corn cobs with parmesan and paprika

VEGETARIAN | PREP + COOK TIME **20 MINUTES** | SERVES **4**

Remove the silks and trim the husks of 4 corn cobs. Cook the corn on a heated oiled grill plate (or barbecue or grill) over a medium heat, turning occasionally, for 10 minutes or until grill marks appear. Drizzle the corn with 1 tablespoon of extra-virgin olive oil; scatter with ½ cup (40g) grated parmesan and sprinkle with 1 teaspoon of smoked paprika. Season with salt and pepper to taste. Serve with lime wedges.

Hokkien mee with beef

PREP + COOK TIME **20 MINUTES** | SERVES **4**

Hokkien mee is a stir-fried noodle dish popular throughout Southeast Asia that has its origins in the cuisine of China's Fujian (Hokkien) province. Deliciously aromatic and rich, it is characterized by the dark, fragrant sauce that the noodles are braised in.

300g thin hokkien noodles (egg noodles)

1 tbsp vegetable oil

700g beef strips

1 medium onion (150g), thinly sliced

2 tsp finely grated fresh ginger

2 garlic cloves, crushed

200g sugar snap peas, trimmed, halved lengthways

1 medium yellow capsicum (pepper) (200g), thinly sliced

1 medium courgette (120g), cut into ribbons

2 cups finely shredded wombok (Chinese leaf)

1/3 cup (80ml) hoisin sauce

1 tbsp dark soy sauce (see tip)

1 tbsp hot water

small fresh mint leaves, to serve

1 Place the noodles in a medium heatproof bowl, cover with boiling water; separate with a fork, drain.

2 Heat half the oil in a wok over a high heat; stir-fry the beef, in batches, until browned. Remove from the wok.

3 Heat the remaining oil in the wok; stir-fry the onion for 2 minutes or until soft. Add the ginger and garlic; stir-fry for about 30 seconds or until fragrant. Add the peas, capsicum, courgette, and wombok; stir-fry until tender.

4 Return the beef to the wok with the noodles, hoisin sauce, soy sauce, and the hot water; stir-fry until heated through. Serve sprinkled with mint.

TIP

Dark soy sauce is almost black in colour; it is rich, with a thicker consistency than other types. Pungent but not particularly salty, it is good for marinating. You can find it in Asian food stores and most supermarkets.

Quinoa "fried rice"

VEGETARIAN | PREP + COOK TIME **25 MINUTES + FREEZING** | SERVES **4**

Quinoa replaces rice in this healthy vegetable stir-fry recipe that scores high in the flavour and nutrition stakes. If you have the time, prepare the quinoa a day before serving; spread it over a tray and refrigerate overnight to dry it out, then continue with the recipe.

1 packet (250g) cooked white quinoa

1 tbsp vegetable oil

4 eggs, lightly beaten

2 tsp sesame oil

2 garlic cloves, thinly sliced

20g piece fresh ginger, cut into matchsticks

1 medium carrot (120g), coarsely grated

1 small red capsicum (pepper) (150g), finely chopped

3/4 cup (90g) frozen baby peas

4 green onions (spring onions), thinly sliced

2 tbsp kecap manis

fresh coriander leaves, to serve

1 Heat 1 teaspoon of the vegetable oil in a wok over a high heat; pour half the egg into the wok, tilt the wok to make a thin omelette. Cook until set. Remove the omelette from the wok; roll it tightly, then slice thinly. Repeat with another 1 teaspoon of the vegetable oil and the remaining egg.

2 Heat the remaining vegetable oil and sesame oil in the wok, add the garlic, ginger, carrot, and capsicum; stir-fry until fragrant. Add the peas and half the green onion; stir-fry until heated through.

3 Add the quinoa and kecap manis to the wok; stir-fry until heated through. Serve the "fried rice" topped with the omelette, coriander, and remaining green onion.

Thai spicy lamb and noodle stir-fry

PREP + COOK TIME **20 MINUTES** | SERVES **4**

Tender lamb, spicy noodles, and a topping of roasted peanuts come together in this delicious take on a Thai stir-fry. Perfect for a family lunch or a simple weekday supper, this dish is ready in just 20 minutes.

200g dried rice noodles

1 tbsp peanut oil

500g lamb backstrap (eye of loin), thinly sliced

3 garlic cloves, crushed

2 small fresh red Thai chillies, finely chopped

2 tbsp fish sauce

2 tbsp dark soy sauce

1 tbsp brown sugar

4 makrut lime leaves, shredded

3 medium tomatoes (450g), finely chopped

fresh Thai basil leaves, to serve

1/4 cup (35g) coarsely chopped roasted unsalted peanuts

1. Cook the noodles according to the directions on the packet; drain.

2. Heat half the oil in a wok over a high heat; stir-fry the lamb, in batches, until browned. Remove from the wok; cover to keep warm.

3. Heat the remaining oil in the wok; stir-fry the garlic and chilli until fragrant. Add the fish sauce, soy sauce, sugar, and three quarters of the lime leaves; stir-fry until combined.

4. Return the lamb to the wok with the noodles and tomato; stir-fry until the tomato starts to soften and is heated through. Serve sprinkled with Thai basil, peanuts, and the remaining lime leaves.

Sweet chilli mussels and hokkien noodles

PESCATARIAN | PREP + COOK TIME **20 MINUTES** | SERVES **2**

Sweet and spicy meets seafood in this light take on Chinese hokkien noodles, where fresh mussels sit on a bed of noodles to create a vibrant dish that's full of flavour and so simple to prepare. Serve with a side of steamed Asian greens, if you like.

440g thin hokkien noodles (egg noodles)

2 tbsp peanut oil

1 shallot (25g), thinly sliced

2 garlic cloves, crushed

4cm piece fresh ginger (20g), grated

1kg pot-ready mussels (see tip)

2 tbsp Chinese cooking wine (shao hsing)

2 green onions (spring onions), thinly sliced

1 fresh long red chilli, thinly sliced

2 tbsp sweet chilli sauce

salt and freshly ground black pepper

fresh coriander leaves, to serve

1 Place the noodles in a medium heatproof bowl, cover with boiling water; separate with a fork, drain.

2 Heat half the oil in a wok; stir-fry the shallot, garlic, and ginger until the shallot softens. Add the mussels and cooking wine; cook, covered, for 5 minutes or until the mussels open. Remove the mussels from the wok; reserve 1/4 cup (60ml) cooking liquid. Remove half of the mussels from their shells.

3 Heat the remaining oil in the wok; stir-fry the green onion and chilli until the green onion softens. Return the mussels to the wok with the noodles, sweet chilli sauce, and reserved cooking liquid; stir-fry until hot. Season with salt and pepper to taste. Serve the stir-fry sprinkled with coriander.

TIP

You can buy cleaned pot-ready mussels from fishmongers. Or, to prepare them at home, scrub the mussels thoroughly with a coarse brush. Remove and discard the beards.

BAKING DISH

Here we have a selection of one-pot wonders baked in the oven, from twists on the classic Sunday roast, to sophisticated fish dishes, and simple weeknight suppers.

Chicken parmigiana bake

PREP + COOK TIME **50 MINUTES** | SERVES **4**

The traditional Italian dish of parmigiana was originally made from layers of aubergine with a tomato sauce and cheese. This popular variation is instead made of chicken layered with vegetables and topped with a crunchy bread and parmesan crumb.

3 cups (750ml) tomato pasta sauce

2 tbsp tomato paste

600g chicken breast fillets, quartered lengthways

1 bunch broccolini (Tenderstem broccoli) (175g), each cut into thirds on the diagonal

200g yellow patty-pan squash, thinly sliced (see tip)

220g bocconcini (mozzarella balls) sliced

3 cups (200g) coarsely torn sourdough bread

3 tsp fennel seeds, toasted, coarsely ground

2 tbsp extra virgin olive oil

$^1/_2$ cup (40g) freshly grated parmesan

salt and freshly ground black pepper

small fresh flat-leaf parsley leaves, to serve

1 Preheat oven to 180°C (160°C fan/350°F/Gas 4).

2 Lightly grease a 10-cup (2.5-litre) rectangular ovenproof dish. Combine the pasta sauce and tomato paste; spoon a third of the sauce mixture over the bottom of the dish. Place half the chicken on the sauce; top with the broccolini, half the squash, and half the mozzarella. Repeat with the remaining sauce mixture, chicken, squash, and mozzarella.

3 Combine the bread, fennel seeds, olive oil, and parmesan in a small bowl, season with salt and pepper to taste; sprinkle over the chicken mixture.

4 Bake for 30 minutes or until the top is lightly browned and the chicken is cooked through. Serve immediately, sprinkled with small fresh flat-leaf parsley leaves, if you like.

TIP

You can use 2 thinly sliced medium courgettes instead of the patty-pan squash, if you prefer.

Feta, basil, and vegetable lamb roasts

PREP + COOK TIME **50 MINUTES** | SERVES **6**

If you're looking for a way to enliven your traditional Sunday roast, this Mediterranean take on a roast dinner is a great one-pot option. Serve with a rocket and mixed tomato salad along with a side of sweet potato chips.

$^1/_2$ cup (100g) drained char-grilled vegetables, coarsely chopped

50g feta, crumbled

2 tbsp coarsely chopped fresh basil

4 lamb mini roasts (1.4kg)

1kg sweet potatoes, cut into chips

cooking-oil spray

1 tbsp coarsely chopped fresh rosemary

salt and freshly ground black pepper

1   Preheat oven to 220°C (200°C fan/425°F/Gas 7).

2   Combine the char-grilled vegetables, feta, and basil in a small bowl.

3   Make a horizontal cut into each lamb roast to make a large pocket, without cutting all the way through. Push the vegetable mixture into the pockets. Tie the lamb at 3cm intervals with kitchen string. Place the lamb on a large oiled oven tray. Add the sweet potato to the tray; spray with oil and sprinkle with the chopped rosemary, season with salt and pepper.

4   Roast the lamb and sweet potato for 35 minutes, or until cooked to your liking. Cover the lamb; stand for 10 minutes. Remove the kitchen string, then slice the lamb thickly.

Fish provençale

PESCATARIAN | PREP + COOK TIME **15 MINUTES** | SERVES **4**

We used perch fillets in this classic fragrant French fish dish, but you can use any firm white fish cutlets, steaks, or fillets you like. Serve with a warm crusty baguette and a radicchio and rocket salad, if you like.

1 garlic clove, thinly sliced

¼ cup (60ml) olive oil

800g firm white fish fillets

salt and freshly ground black pepper

500g tomatoes, cut into wedges

1 tbsp finely chopped fresh rosemary

1 tbsp fresh lemon thyme leaves

⅓ cup (80ml) dry white wine

⅓ cup (80ml) fish stock

6 green onions (spring onions), trimmed, cut into thirds

⅓ cup (55g) pitted mixed olives

2 pickled jalapeño chillies, halved lengthways

1 Preheat the oven to 200°C (180°C fan/400°F/Gas 6).

2 Place the garlic and the olive oil in a small bowl. Mix until combined. Drizzle 2 tablespoons of the garlic oil in the bottom of a 23 x 30cm baking dish.

3 Season the fish on both sides with salt and pepper. Lay the fillets in the baking dish, then top with the tomato, rosemary, and thyme. Pour the white wine, stock, and the remaining olive oil over the top of the fish and tomatoes. Top with the green onions, olives, and pickled jalapeños.

4 Bake for 20–25 minutes, depending on the thickness of the fillets, until the fish is cooked through and the tomatoes are blistered. If the fish cooks too quickly, you can remove it and return the tomatoes and onions to the oven for another 5 minutes.

Vegetable and ricotta lasagne

VEGETARIAN | PREP + COOK TIME **50 MINUTES** | SERVES **6**

Instead of breaking the pasta into long strips, you could simply break it all into bite-sized pieces; mix the pieces into the spinach and tomato sauce mixture, sprinkle over the cheese, and cook the lasagne as directed.

1 tbsp olive oil

1 large onion (200g), finely chopped

2 garlic cloves, crushed

250g packet lasagne sheets
(you need 11 sheets)

150g baby spinach leaves

500g antipasto vegetable mix

700g bottled tomato passata

1 cup (250ml) water

1¹/₂ cups (360g) firm ricotta, crumbled

1¹/₂ cups (150g) coarsely grated mozzarella

fresh basil leaves, to serve

1   Heat the olive oil in a 12-cup (3-litre) flameproof baking dish (see tip) over a medium heat; cook the onion and garlic, stirring, until the onion softens.

2   Meanwhile, break the lasagne sheets lengthways into strips; put the long strips aside, save any small broken pieces. Sprinkle the small broken pasta pieces, spinach, and antipasto into the dish with the onion; mix gently to combine.

3   Pour the combined passata and water into the dish; insert the long pasta strips into the mixture. Sprinkle with both cheeses. Bring to the boil over a high heat; reduce the heat to low; Cover with foil; simmer, for 20 minutes or until the pasta is tender.

4   Preheat grill.

5   Remove the foil. Grill the lasagne for 5 minutes or until the cheese is browned. Cover, stand for 5 minutes before serving. Sprinkle with basil leaves.

TIP

You can use a large round deep frying pan instead, with a base measurement of 28cm and a domed lid; cover the handle with aluminium foil to protect it from the heat of the grill.

Portuguese piri piri chicken

PREP + COOK TIME **35 MINUTES** | SERVES **4**

If you and your family are not used to hot and spicy tastes, reduce the amount of chilli in the piri piri sauce, adding only enough to suit your heat tolerance. Removing the seeds and membranes from chillies also lessens the heat level.

2 medium Desiree potatoes (400g)

1.4kg butterflied chicken (see tip)

$^1/_3$ cup (80ml) vegetable oil

piri piri sauce

6 fresh long red chillies

1 tsp finely grated lemon rind

2 tbsp lemon juice

4 garlic cloves, halved

2 tsp sweet paprika

$^1/_4$ cup (5g) coarsely chopped fresh oregano

$^1/_2$ cup (125ml) olive oil

salt

1 Preheat oven to 200°C (180°C fan/400°F/Gas 6).

2 Make the piri piri sauce. Discard the seeds from 3 of the chillies, then coarsely chop all the chillies; process with the remaining ingredients until well combined. Season well with salt.

3 Prick the potatoes all over with a fork. Microwave on HIGH (100%) for about 3 minutes or until the potatoes are tender. Cut into 4cm pieces.

4 Meanwhile, rub $^1/_3$ cup (80ml) of the piri piri sauce over both sides of the chicken. Heat the oil in a large flameproof roasting pan over a medium-high heat. Cook the chicken, skin-side down, for 5 minutes. Turn the chicken over. Add the potato slices to the pan; cook for a further 5 minutes, turning the potato until golden. Transfer the pan to the oven; roast the chicken for 15 minutes or until the juices run clear when the thickest part of the thigh is pierced.

5 Place the potato and chicken on a platter; accompany with the remaining piri piri sauce and a green salad, if you like.

TIP

Ask the butcher to butterfly the chicken for you. Or, to do it yourself, use a large heavy, flat-bladed knife to cut along each side of the backbone; discard the bone. Open the chicken out and press down on the breast bone to flatten. Or you can use other cuts of chicken on the bone, such as wings, cutlets, and marylands (legs), if you prefer.

Grains

Quinoa and couscous are great additions to many one-pot dishes, and being rich in minerals and antioxidants they offer a healthy alternative to more carb-heavy sides. Serve plain or bring in the flavour combinations that best match your main dish.

Basic quinoa

VEGAN | PREP + COOK TIME **20 MINUTES** | SERVES **4**

Rinse 1 cup (200g) tricoloured quinoa in a sieve under cold running water. Place the quinoa and 2 cups (500ml) water in a medium saucepan; bring to the boil. Reduce the heat to low; cook, covered, for 15 minutes or until tender. Drain; cool slightly. Season with salt and pepper to taste.

Lemon pistachio couscous

VEGAN | PREP + COOK TIME **15 MINUTES** | SERVES **4**

Combine 1 cup couscous, $3/4$ cup (190ml) boiling water, 2 teaspoons of finely grated lemon rind, and $1/4$ cup (60ml) lemon juice in a heatproof bowl. Cover; stand for 5 minutes or until the liquid is absorbed; fluff with a fork. Meanwhile, cook $1/2$ cup (70g) pistachios in a dry heated frying pan until fragrant; remove the nuts from the pan, chop coarsely. Heat 2 teaspoons of olive oil in the same pan, add 1 crushed garlic clove and 1 finely chopped small red onion; cook, stirring, until the onion softens. Fluff the couscous then stir through the pistachios, onion mixture and $1/2$ cup (4g) shredded fresh mint.

Preserved lemon and olive couscous

VEGAN | PREP + COOK TIME **15 MINUTES** | SERVES **6**

Combine $11/4$ cups (250g) couscous, $11/4$ cups (300ml) boiling water and 1 tablespoon of olive oil in a heatproof bowl, cover; stand for 5 minutes or until the water is absorbed, fluffing with a fork occasionally. Stir 400g can drained and rinsed chickpeas, $1/2$ cup (80g) coarsely chopped pitted green olives, 2 tablespoons of lemon juice, 3 thinly sliced green onions (spring onions), 2 tablespoons of finely chopped fresh flat-leaf parsley, and 1 tablespoon thinly sliced preserved lemon rind into the couscous. Season with salt and pepper to taste.

Pine nut and parsley quinoa

VEGAN | PREP + COOK TIME **20 MINUTES** | SERVES **4**

Place 1 cup (220g) red quinoa and 2 cups (500ml) water in a medium saucepan and bring to the boil. Reduce the heat to low; cook, covered, for 12 minutes or until the water is absorbed and the quinoa is tender. Stir in $1/3$ cup (50g) toasted pine nuts, 2 teaspoons of finely grated lemon rind, 2 tablespoons of lemon juice, and $1/2$ cup (10g) finely chopped fresh flat-leaf parsley; season with salt and pepper to taste.

One-pan sausage bake

PREP + COOK TIME **40 MINUTES** | SERVES **4**

This hearty bake combines sausages and roasted vegetables and is served alongside creamy polenta to make a great midweek meal for all the family. Use whatever flavour sausage you prefer and serve with a mixed-leaf salad, if you like.

8 thick beef sausages

2 medium yellow capsicums (peppers) (400g), thickly sliced

1 small red onion (100g), cut into wedges

salt and freshly ground black pepper

375g cherry tomatoes

500g ready-made polenta

1/4 cup (20g) finely grated parmesan

small fresh basil leaves, to serve

1 Preheat oven to 200°C (180°C fan/400°F/Gas 6).

2 Heat a large flameproof baking dish over high heat. Cook the sausages until browned all over. Add the capsicum and onion; season with salt and pepper.

3 Transfer the dish to the oven; roast for 15 minutes. Add the tomatoes, roast for a further 15 minutes or until the sausages are cooked through and the vegetables are tender.

4 Meanwhile, heat the polenta according to packet directions. Stir in parmesan until well combined; season with salt and pepper to taste.

5 Serve the sausage and vegetable bake with the creamy polenta. Sprinkle with basil leaves.

Creamy chicken and corn burritos

PREP + COOK TIME **35 MINUTES** | SERVES **4**

Using canned corn and pre-cooked chicken, this is a simple, fuss-free, quick to prepare meal to whip up on a busy weekday. It's also a great way use up any leftover roast chicken. Serve with a tomato and avocado salad.

1¼ cups (20g) loosely packed fresh coriander leaves

310g can corn kernels (sweetcorn), drained, rinsed

3 cups (480g) shredded cooked chicken (see tip)

2 cups (240g) coarsely grated cheddar

1 cup (240g) light sour cream

1 garlic clove, crushed

½ tsp cayenne pepper

salt and freshly ground black pepper

8 x 20cm flour tortillas

lime halves, to serve

1 Preheat oven to 220°C (200°C fan/425°F/Gas 7). Oil a large ovenproof dish.

2 Coarsely chop ¼ cup (4g) of the coriander. Combine the corn, chopped coriander, chicken, 1 cup (120g) of the cheddar, the sour cream, garlic, and half the cayenne pepper in a medium bowl; season with salt and pepper to taste.

3 To make the burritos, divide the chicken mixture evenly among the tortillas; roll to enclose the filling, folding in the sides. Place the burritos in the dish; sprinkle with the remaining cheddar and cayenne pepper. Bake for 25 minutes or until lightly browned.

TIP

A large (900g) chicken should give 3 cups (480g) of shredded chicken meat.

Baked lamb chops with capsicum and tomato

PREP + COOK TIME **45 MINUTES** | SERVES **4**

Tender juicy lamb chops and beautifully roasted vegetables make a simple yet satisfying dish perfect for a midweek dinner. Serve with mashed potato and steamed greens such as peas, broccoli, and beans.

4 lamb forequarter chops (760g)

2 medium yellow capsicums (peppers) (400g), thickly sliced

375g cherry tomatoes on the vine

1 small red onion (100g), cut into wedges

micro herbs, to serve

1 Preheat oven to 200°C (180°C fan/400°F/Gas 6).

2 Heat a large flameproof baking dish over a high heat. Cook the lamb until browned all over. Add the capsicum, tomato, and onion to the dish.

3 Transfer the dish to the oven; roast for 30 minutes or until the lamb is cooked through and the vegetables are tender.

4 Serve the lamb and vegetables sprinkled with micro herbs.

Spicy courgette and ricotta pasta shells

VEGETARIAN | PREP + COOK TIME **1 HOUR** | SERVES **4**

In this delicious twist on an Italian classic, pasta shells are stuffed with courgette and ricotta and baked in a rich, spicy tomato sauce. Serve with a green salad and fresh crusty bread, if you like.

3 medium courgettes (360g)

1^1/$_3$ cups (320g) firm ricotta

^{3}/$_4$ cup (60g) finely grated parmesan (make sure it doesn't contain animal rennet)

^{1}/$_3$ cup (50g) roasted pine nuts

3 egg yolks

2 garlic cloves, crushed

1 tbsp fresh lemon thyme leaves

^{1}/$_2$ tsp dried chilli flakes

salt and freshly ground black pepper

5 cups (1.3kg) bottled tomato pasta sauce

250g large pasta shells

1 tbsp fresh lemon thyme leaves, extra

1 Preheat oven to 200°C (180°C fan/400°F/Gas 6). Oil a shallow 10-cup (2.5-litre) ovenproof dish.

2 Coarsely grate the courgette. Combine the courgette, ricotta, parmesan, pine nuts, egg yolks, garlic, lemon thyme, and chilli in a medium bowl; season with salt and pepper.

3 Spread the pasta sauce into the dish; season with salt and pepper. Spoon the courgette mixture into the uncooked pasta shells; place in the dish.

4 Cover the dish with foil; bake for 30 minutes. Uncover; bake for 15 minutes or until the pasta is tender and the cheese is lightly browned. Serve the pasta sprinkled with the extra lemon thyme leaves.

TIP

You can make this dish up to 1 day ahead of time. Reheat at 180°C (160°C fan/350°F/Gas 4) for 25 minutes or until heated through with the cheese melted.

Chicken and broccoli pie with pangrattato topping

PREP + COOK TIME **1 HOUR** | SERVES **4**

Pangrattato is Italian for breadcrumbs and is known as "poor man's parmesan" though it's just as delicious once toasted in garlic and oil, and it brings a wonderful texture to dishes. Our more extravagant bread topping also includes parmesan.

40g butter

2 tbsp plain flour

2 cups (500ml) milk

1/2 cup (60g) coarsely grated cheddar

2 1/2 cups (400g) shredded barbecued chicken

500g broccoli, cut into small florets

salt and freshly ground black pepper

4 slices sourdough bread (280g)

1 tbsp olive oil

1 garlic clove, crushed

1 tbsp finely grated lemon rind

2 tbsp finely chopped fresh flat-leaf parsley

1/2 cup (40g) finely grated parmesan

fresh flat-leaf parsley leaves, extra, to serve

1   Preheat oven to 220°C (200°C fan/425°F/Gas 7).

2   In a large ovenproof dish, melt the butter and add the flour; cook, stirring, for 2 minutes or until the mixture bubbles and thickens. Gradually stir in the milk; cook, stirring, until the mixture boils and thickens. Stir in the cheddar, chicken, and broccoli; season with salt and pepper. Spoon the mixture into the dish.

3   Tear the bread into pieces; combine the bread with the remaining ingredients in a medium bowl. Sprinkle the bread mixture on top of the chicken mixture. Bake for 30 minutes or until lightly browned. Stand for 5 minutes before serving, sprinkle with the extra parsley.

Moroccan fish and chips

PREP + COOK TIME **1 HOUR** | SERVES **4**

Spices and sweet potatoes bring a whole new dimension to this Moroccan take
on a classic. You can use any firm white fish fillets you like here. Serve with
a cucumber and coriander salad, if you like.

³/₄ cup (12g) fresh coriander leaves

¹/₄ cup (60ml) olive oil

2 tbsp lemon juice

6 garlic cloves, quartered

2 tsp sweet paprika

¹/₂ tsp ground cumin

¹/₄ tsp cayenne pepper

¹/₂ cup (125ml) chicken stock

1kg sweet potatoes, cut into thick wedges

1 cup (70g) stale breadcrumbs

2 tbsp finely chopped fresh flat-leaf parsley

2 tsp finely grated lemon rind

salt and freshly ground black pepper

4 x 200g firm white fish fillets

¹/₄ cup (4g) fresh coriander leaves, extra

lemon cheeks, to serve

1 Preheat oven to 200°C (180°C fan/400°F/Gas 6). Oil an 8-cup (2-litre)
ovenproof dish.

2 Blend or process the coriander, 2 tablespoons of the olive oil, lemon
juice, garlic, and spices until smooth; combine the spice paste, stock,
and sweet potato in the prepared dish. Roast for 20 minutes.

3 Combine the breadcrumbs, parsley, lemon rind, and remaining oil in a
small bowl; season with salt and pepper. Press the mixture onto the fish.

4 Remove the dish from the oven. Place the fish on top of the sweet potato;
return to the oven, roast for 20 minutes or until the sweet potato is
golden and the fish is just cooked through. Stand for 5 minutes before
serving, sprinkled with the extra coriander leaves and accompanied
with lemon cheeks.

TIP

This dish is best served the day you make it.
To reheat, separate the fish from the potatoes.
Warm the cooked fish gently on the stove. Heat the
potatoes in the oven at 180°C (160°C fan/350°F/Gas 4)
for 20–25 minutes.

Dukkah-crusted lamb cutlets and roasted cauliflower

PREP + COOK TIME **55 MINUTES** | SERVES **4**

Dukkah is an Egyptian spice blend made with roasted nuts and aromatic spices. It is available from major supermarkets and delicatessens. Serve this with your favourite store-bought baba ganoush or hummus instead of the tahini herb dressing, if you like.

1 small cauliflower (1kg), trimmed, cut into 1.5cm florets

300g small sweet potatoes, sliced

$^1/_4$ cup (60ml) olive oil

salt and freshly ground black pepper

$^2/_3$ cup (90g) dukkah

2 tbsp pomegranate molasses or balsamic glaze

12 french-trimmed lamb cutlets (600g)

olive-oil spray

1 tbsp fresh flat-leaf parsley leaves

1 tbsp fresh mint leaves

$^1/_4$ cup (20g) flaked natural almonds, lightly toasted

100g rocket, mixed salad leaves, or watercress

1 medium lemon (140g), cut into wedges

$^1/_4$ tsp smoked paprika

tahini herb dressing

$^1/_4$ cup (125ml) tahini

$^1/_4$ cup (60ml) lemon juice

1 garlic clove, crushed

$^1/_4$ cup (60ml) cold water

2 tbsp finely chopped fresh coriander

2 tbsp finely chopped fresh mint

1 Preheat oven to 220°C (200°C fan/425°F/Gas 7). Line three large oven trays with baking paper.

2 Place the cauliflower and sweet potato on two oven trays; drizzle with half the olive oil, season with salt and pepper. Roast for 20 minutes or until golden and tender.

3 Meanwhile, place the dukkah in a shallow bowl. Combine the pomegranate molasses with the remaining olive oil; rub onto the lamb, season with salt and pepper. Press the lamb firmly onto the dukkah to coat both sides; place on the remaining lined oven tray. Spray the lamb lightly with oil; roast for 12 minutes for medium-rare or until golden and cooked as desired.

4 Make the tahini herb dressing. Combine all the ingredients in a small bowl until emulsified; season with salt and pepper to taste.

5 Arrange the cauliflower and sweet potato on a platter; top with the lamb, herbs, and almonds. Serve with rocket, lemon wedges, and the tahini herb dressing, sprinkled with paprika.

Smoky pork enchiladas

PREP + COOK TIME **25 MINUTES** | SERVES **4**

Fresh and flavoursome, this Mexican-inspired dish is smoky, spicy, and covered in a blanket of cheese – what's not to love? Simple to prepare and quick to cook it makes a perfect midweek dinner. Serve with a simple green or cabbage salad on the side.

1 tbsp olive oil

500g minced pork

1 medium red onion (170g), finely chopped

4 garlic cloves, crushed

1 fresh long green chilli, chopped

1 tbsp smoked paprika

2 x 400g cans chopped tomatoes

1 tbsp lime juice

salt and freshly ground black pepper

8 x 20cm flour tortillas

2 cups (240g) coarsely grated cheddar

fresh coriander leaves, to serve

lime wedges, to serve

1 Preheat oven to 220°C (200°C fan/425°F/Gas 7).

2 Heat the olive oil in a 20cm x 30cm shallow flameproof dish over a high heat. Cook the pork, onion, garlic, chilli, and paprika, stirring, for 5 minutes or until browned. Add 1 can of tomatoes; cook for 1 minute. Stir in the lime juice; season with salt and pepper to taste.

3 Spread the tortillas flat on a work surface. Spoon the mince mixture equally onto the centre of each tortilla, then sprinkle 1 cup (120g) of the cheddar equally over the mince mixture; fold the tortillas to enclose the filling. Clean the emptied dish.

4 Place the filled tortillas, join-side down, in a single layer in the same dish. Spoon over the remaining can of tomatoes, leaving the ends of the tortilla exposed; sprinkle with the remaining cheddar.

5 Bake for 15 minutes or until golden. Sprinkle the enchiladas with coriander; serve with lime wedges.

Tasty toppings

Take your one-pot dish to another level with one of these tasty toppings. Mix and match according to your flavour preferences and whatever pairs best with the meal you've cooked. Use them to elevate a simple supper, bringing in a contrasting texture and a depth of flavour.

Broccoli pesto

VEGETARIAN | PREP + COOK TIME **15 MINUTES** | SERVES **4**

Cook 100g chopped broccoli in a small saucepan of boiling water for 2 minutes; drain. Refresh in cold water; drain well. Process the broccoli, 1 crushed garlic clove, $1^{1}/_{2}$ tablespoons of toasted pine nuts, $1^{1}/_{2}$ tablespoons of grated parmesan (make sure it doesn't contain animal rennet), and $1^{1}/_{2}$ tablespoons of coarsely chopped basil until finely chopped. With the motor operating, gradually pour in $^{1}/_{4}$ cup (60ml) extra virgin olive oil; process until combined. Season with salt and pepper to taste. Scatter with extra pine nuts and basil leaves, if you like.

Spiced lime yogurt

VEGETARIAN | PREP + COOK TIME **5 MINUTES** | MAKES **$^{1}/_{2}$ CUP (140G)**

Stir $^{1}/_{2}$ cup (140g) Greek-style yogurt, 1 crushed garlic clove, 1 tablespoon of lime juice, and a pinch of cayenne pepper in a small bowl; season with salt and pepper to taste. Top with finely grated lime rind and a little extra cayenne pepper, if you like.

Almond gremolata

VEGAN | PREP + COOK TIME **10 MINUTES** | MAKES **1 CUP (160G)**

Coarsely chop $^{1}/_{2}$ cup (80g) roasted natural almonds. Combine the almonds in a medium bowl with 1 crushed garlic clove, 1 tablespoon of grated lemon rind, and $^{1}/_{2}$ cup (10g) chopped fresh flat-leaf parsley.

Chunky guacamole

VEGAN | PREP + COOK TIME **15 MINUTES** | SERVES **4**

Combine 1 coarsely mashed large avocado, 1 thinly sliced green onion (spring onion), 2 tablespoons of chopped fresh coriander leaves, 100g halved or quartered grape (cherry) tomatoes, and 2 tablespoons of lime juice in a small bowl. Season with salt and pepper to taste. Top with extra coriander leaves, if you like.

Salami and olive cacciatore

PREP + COOK TIME **35 MINUTES** | SERVES **6**

Rich and rustic, chicken cacciatore is an Italian classic. If you can find pitted Sicilian
green olives, use them here, otherwise warn your guests about the pits in the olives.
Serve with crusty bread, if you like.

2 tsp olive oil

6 x 180g chicken thigh cutlets, skin on

10 baby potatoes (400g), sliced into thin rounds

130g sliced salami, chopped

1 medium onion (150g), thinly sliced

6 garlic cloves, crushed

$1/2$ tsp fennel seeds, crushed (see tip)

$1/2$ cup (125ml) dry white wine

400g can chopped tomatoes

1 cup (250ml) chicken stock

$3/4$ cup (200g) whole Sicilian green olives

5 sprigs fresh thyme

5 sprigs fresh basil

$1/3$ cup (25g) finely grated parmesan

$1/2$ cup (10g) small fresh basil leaves, torn

1 Preheat oven to 220°C (200°C fan/425°F/Gas 7).

2 Heat the olive oil in a large casserole dish over a medium-high heat,
add the chicken, skin-side down; cook for 3 minutes each side or until
browned. Remove from the pan.

3 Add the potato, salami, onion, garlic, and fennel to the same pan; cook,
stirring, for about 4 minutes or until the onion is golden.

4 Add the wine to the pan; stir to combine. Add the tomatoes, stock, olives,
thyme and basil sprigs, and chicken; bring to the boil. Transfer to the
oven; bake for 20 minutes or until the chicken is cooked through.

5 Sprinkle the cacciatore with parmesan and torn basil leaves.

TIP

To crush the fennel seeds, place them on a chopping
board and press down on them with the base of a
clean heavy-based frying pan or saucepan.

Whole snapper, potato wedges, and horseradish mayo

PESCATARIAN | PREP + COOK TIME **50 MINUTES** | SERVES **2**

Fresh zesty fish and potato wedges are roasted to perfection in this tempting twist on a classic. Serve with a hit of horseradish mayo and a fragrant shaved fennel and mixed herb salad, if you like.

400g potatoes

6 garlic cloves

2 tbsp olive oil

salt and freshly ground black pepper

2 whole baby snapper (600g), cleaned

1 medium lemon (140g), thinly sliced

$1/3$ cup (8g) loosely packed fresh dill sprigs

2 tsp drained, rinsed capers

$1/4$ cup (75g) mayonnaise

2 tsp horseradish cream

lemon cheeks, to serve

1 Preheat oven to 240°C (220 °C fan/475°F/Gas 9).

2 Wash the unpeeled potatoes; cut into wedges. Combine the potato, unpeeled garlic, and 1 tablespoon of the olive oil in a large baking dish; season with salt and pepper. Roast for 20 minutes.

3 Meanwhile, fill the fish cavities with lemon and $1/4$ cup (6g) of the dill; season with salt and pepper. Place the fish on top of the potato; drizzle with the remaining olive oil. Roast for 25 minutes or until the fish and potato are cooked through.

4 Meanwhile, finely chop the remaining dill and capers. Combine the dill and capers with the mayonnaise and horseradish cream in a small bowl.

5 Serve the roast fish and potato with the horseradish mayonnaise and lemon cheeks.

Walnut dukkah baked ocean trout

PESCATARIAN | PREP + COOK TIME **35 MINUTES** | SERVES **6**

Buy a whole ocean trout side fillet for this if you can; you could use the trimmed trout belly to make a fish tartare or ceviche. Alternatively, use four 200g ocean trout fillets or salmon fillets instead; roast for 5 minutes or until cooked as desired.

150g turkish bread

45g lemon dukkah (see tip)

1/3 cup (35g) walnuts, coarsely chopped

2 cups (20g) fresh flat-leaf parsley leaves, coarsely chopped

2 tbsp dried currants

2 tbsp extra virgin olive oil

2 tbsp Greek-style yogurt

1 tbsp tahini

1kg piece skinless boneless ocean trout fillet (or salmon fillet)

salt and freshly ground black pepper

800g grape (cherry) tomatoes, halved

60g watercress sprigs

lemon wedges, to serve

tahini-yogurt sauce

2 tbsp Greek-style yogurt

1 tbsp tahini

2 tbsp lemon juice

2 tsp finely chopped fresh flat-leaf parsley

1 Preheat oven to 200°C (180°C fan/400°F/Gas 6). Line a large roasting pan or oven tray with baking paper.

2 Process the bread to medium-sized coarse crumbs; transfer to a medium bowl. Add the dukkah, walnuts, parsley, currants, and olive oil; season with salt and pepper to taste. Stir well so that the oil coats the ingredients. Combine the yogurt and tahini in a small bowl.

3 Pat the fish dry with paper towel. Trim the belly; discard or reserve for another use. Place the fish on the tray; season with salt and pepper. Brush the yogurt mixture over the fish. Top with the breadcrumb mixture, patting down firmly to coat.

4 Roast the fish for 15 minutes or until the crumb crust is golden and the fish is still pink in the centre, or continue until cooked as desired.

5 Meanwhile, make the tahini-yogurt sauce. Combine the yogurt and tahini in a small bowl. Add the lemon juice and parsley; combine well. Season with salt and pepper to taste.

6 Serve the trout with the tahini-yogurt sauce, tomatoes, watercress, and lemon wedges.

TIP

Dukkah is a Middle Eastern spice and nut blend usually made of hazelnuts, almonds, coriander, cumin, and other spices sold in gourmet or international groceries. You can substitute za'atar for the dukkah.

Paprika lamb and chickpea tray bake

PREP + COOK TIME **45 MINUTES** | SERVES **4**

Warm and smoky with a zesty finish, this lamb tray bake brings together Mediterranean flavours in a simple yet satisfying supper for all the family. Serve with a mixed-leaf salad and crusty bread, if you like.

8 lamb forequarter chops (1.5kg)

1 tbsp ground turmeric

2 tsp smoked paprika

2 tsp finely grated lemon rind

1 garlic clove, crushed

$1/3$ cup (80ml) olive oil

salt and freshly ground black pepper

500g grape (cherry) tomatoes, on the vine

400g can chickpeas, drained, rinsed

$1/3$ cup (20g) loosely packed fresh flat-leaf parsley leaves

1 tbsp lemon juice

lemon wedges, to serve

1 Preheat oven to (200°C fan/425°F/Gas 7). Line a baking dish with baking paper.

2 Combine the lamb, turmeric, paprika, lemon rind, garlic, and half the olive oil in the prepared dish; season with salt and pepper. Spread into a single layer; roast for 15 minutes.

3 Remove the dish from the oven, add the tomatoes; drizzle with half the remaining olive oil, season with salt and pepper. Return to the oven; roast for 15 minutes or until the lamb is cooked as desired.

4 Just before serving, add the chickpeas, parsley, lemon juice, and remaining olive oil to the dish. Serve with lemon wedges.

Pork, crackling, and pear tray bake

PREP + COOK TIME **45 MINUTES + STANDING** | SERVES **4**

Use two quartered granny smith apples instead of the pears, if you like. Serve this dish with kale mashed potatoes (see page 70) for a satisfying weeknight dinner. Creamy polenta also tastes great with this recipe.

4 x 300g pork loin chops (see tip)

salt and freshly ground black pepper

1 tbsp olive oil

1 medium garlic bulb, broken into clusters

4 small pears (720g), halved lengthways

8 fresh sage sprigs

1 Preheat oven to 200°C (180°C fan/400°F/Gas 6). Oil and line a large roasting pan with baking paper.

2 Remove the rind from the pork, score; cut the rind in half lengthways. Season the rind and chops generously. Place the rind and garlic in a lined pan; roast for 15 minutes or until the rind is crisp and the garlic is golden. Transfer to a paper towel-lined plate.

3 Add the pork to the pan; roast for 2 minutes. Turn the pork; add the pears and sage. Roast for 10 minutes or until both the pork and pears are tender and browned; stand, covered loosely with foil, for 10 minutes. Discard the excess fat from the pan, keeping any pan juices.

4 Serve with kale mashed potatoes or creamy polenta topped with the pork and pear with the pan juices, crackling, and roasted garlic; sprinkle with the sliced green onion.

TIP

You can instead use pork loin steaks if you'd like to eliminate the bones in the dish.

Baked prawns with feta

PESCATARIAN | PREP + COOK TIME **45 MINUTES** | SERVES **4**

This punchy prawn and feta bake is so simple to rustle up. Succulent prawns in a rich tomato sauce are sprinkled with crumbled feta for a perfect seafood supper. Serve with a leafy green salad and crusty bread, if you like.

1kg uncooked medium king prawns

1 tbsp olive oil

1 medium onion (150g), thinly sliced

2 garlic cloves, crushed

400g tomato passata

a few drops Tabasco

salt and freshly ground black pepper

100g feta, crumbled

2 tbsp coarsely chopped fresh flat-leaf parsley

fresh crusty bread, to serve

1   Preheat the oven to 180°C (160°C fan/350°F/Gas 4).

2   Shell and devein the prawns, leaving the tails intact.

3   Combine the prawns, olive oil, onion, garlic, passata, and Tabasco in a 1-litre (4-cup) ovenproof dish; season with salt and pepper. Sprinkle with the feta. Bake for 30 minutes or until the prawns are cooked through.

4   Sprinkle the prawns with parsley; serve with bread.

Roast chicken with preserved lemon

PREP + COOK TIME **1½ HOURS + REFRIGERATION** | SERVES **6**

We used brine-cured Sicilian olives for their lovely flavour and texture, but you could use kalamata olives instead. Serve with steamed giant couscous mixed with coarsely chopped fresh flat-leaf parsley.

2 wedges preserved lemon (see tip)

6 garlic cloves, crushed

1½ tsp ground ginger

1 tsp ground cumin

1 tsp sweet paprika

1 tsp chilli flakes

½ tsp ground turmeric

2 tbsp olive oil

6 chicken marylands (legs) (2kg)

¼ tsp saffron threads

1 cup (250ml) boiling water

4 medium onions (600g), thinly sliced

150g pitted Sicilian green olives

fresh coriander leaves, to serve

1 Remove the flesh from the preserved lemon; discard the flesh. Rinse the rind well. Finely chop the rind of 1 wedge; thinly slice the rind of the other wedge. Refrigerate the sliced rind until required. Combine the chopped lemon rind, garlic, spices, and half the olive oil in a large bowl with the chicken. Cover; refrigerate for 3 hours or overnight.

2 Preheat oven to 180°C (160°C fan/350°F/Gas 4).

3 Combine the saffron and water in a small heatproof bowl.

4 Heat the remaining olive oil in a large roasting pan over a medium heat; cook the chicken, in batches, until browned both sides. Remove from the pan.

5 Cook the onion in the same pan for 5 minutes or until softened. Add the saffron mixture; bring to the boil. Spread the onion mixture evenly over the bottom of the dish; arrange the chicken on top, in a single layer.

6 Transfer the pan to the oven; roast the chicken for 35 minutes. Add the thinly sliced rind and olives; roast for a further 25 minutes or until the chicken is cooked through.

7 Just before serving the chicken, top with coriander.

TIP

Only the rind of the preserved lemon is used. Rinse the rind well before using.

Conversion chart

A note on Australian measures

- One Australian metric measuring cup holds approximately 250ml.

- One Australian metric tablespoon holds 20ml.

- One Australian metric teaspoon holds 5ml.

- The difference between one country's measuring cups and another's is within a two-or three-teaspoon variance, and should not affect your cooking results.

- North America, New Zealand, and the United Kingdom use a 15ml tablespoon.

Using measures in this book

- All cup and spoon measurements are level.

- The most accurate way of measuring dry ingredients is to weigh them.

- When measuring liquids, use a clear glass or plastic jug with metric markings.

- We use large eggs with an average weight of 60g.

Dry measures

metric	imperial
15g	$1/2$oz
30g	1oz
60g	2oz
90g	3oz
125g	4oz ($1/4$lb)
155g	5oz
185g	6oz
220g	7oz
250g	8oz ($1/2$lb)
280g	9oz
315g	10oz
345g	11oz
375g	12oz ($3/4$lb)
410g	13oz
440g	14oz
470g	15oz
500g	16oz (1lb)
750g	24oz ($1^{1}/2$lb)
1kg	32oz (2lb)

Liquid measures

metric	imperial
30ml	1 fluid oz
60ml	2 fluid oz
100ml	3 fluid oz
125ml	4 fluid oz
150ml	5 fluid oz
190ml	6 fluid oz
250ml	8 fluid oz
300ml	10 fluid oz
500ml	16 fluid oz
600ml	20 fluid oz
1000ml (1 litre)	$1^{3}/4$ pints

Length measures

metric	imperial
3mm	$1/8$in
6mm	$1/4$in
1cm	$1/2$in
2cm	$3/4$in
2.5cm	1in
5cm	2in
6cm	$2^{1}/2$in
8cm	3in
10cm	4in
13cm	5in
15cm	6in
18cm	7in
20cm	8in
22cm	9in
25cm	10in
28cm	11in
30cm	12in (1ft)

Oven temperatures

The oven temperatures in this book are for conventional ovens; if you have a fan-forced oven, decrease the temperature by 10–20 degrees.

	°C (Celsius)	°F (Fahrenheit)
Very slow	120	250
Slow	150	300
Moderately slow	160	325
Moderate	180	350
Moderately hot	200	400
Hot	220	425
Very hot	240	475

Index

Acknowledgments

DK would like to thank Sophia Young, Simone
Aquilina, Amanda Chebatte, Georgia Moore,
and Joe Revill for their assistance in making
this book.

The Australian Women's Weekly Test Kitchen in
Sydney, Australia has developed, tested and
photographed the recipes in this book.

Photographers Ben Dearnly, Cath Muscat,
Benito Martin, James Moffatt.

Stylists Vivien Walsh, Annette Forrest, Kate
Brown, Bernadette Smithies, Olivia Blackmore

Photochefs Charlotte Binns-Mcdonald, Alice
Storey, Claire Dickson-Smith, Rebecca Truda,
Peta Dent, Carly Sophia Taylor, Elizabeth Fiducia,
Rebecca Lyall.